Heaven in Ordinary

George Herbert and His Writings

Other titles in the *Canterbury Studies in Spiritual Theology*

Before the King's Majesty: Lancelot Andrewes and His Writings
Edited by Raymond Chapman

Firmly I Believe: An Oxford Movement Reader
Edited by Raymond Chapman

Glory Descending: Michael Ramsey and His Writings
Douglas Dales, John Habgood, Geoffrey Rowell and
Rowan Williams

Holiness and Happiness: Thomas Traherne and His Writings
Edited by Denise Inge

The Sacramental Life: Gregory Dix and His Writings
Edited by Simon Jones

The Truth Seeking Heart: Austin Farrer and His Writings
Edited by Ann Loades and Robert MacSwain

To Build Christ's Kingdom: F. D. Maurice and His Writings
Edited by Jeremy Morris

CANTERBURY STUDIES IN SPIRITUAL THEOLOGY

Heaven in Ordinary

George Herbert and His Writings

Edited and Introduced by
Philip Sheldrake

CANTERBURY
PRESS
Norwich

© Philip Sheldrake 2009

First published in 2009 by the Canterbury Press Norwich
Editorial office
13–17 Long Lane,
London, EC1A 9PN, UK

Canterbury Press is an imprint of Hymns Ancient and Modern Ltd
(a registered charity)
St Mary's Works, St Mary's Plain,
Norwich, NR3 3BH, UK

www.scm-canterburypress.co.uk

British Library Cataloguing in Publication data

A catalogue record for this book is available
from the British Library

978 1 85311 948 4

Typeset by Regent Typesetting, London
Printed in the UK by
CPI William Clowes, Beccles, NR34 7TL

Contents

Preface

I first read George Herbert's poetic collection *The Temple* thirty years ago and immediately fell in love with it. Subsequently I went on to study *The Country Parson* while teaching Christian spirituality at Heythrop College, University of London. These studies, combined with five years (1992–7) as tutor and Director of Pastoral Studies at the Church of England theological college, Westcott House Cambridge, enabled me as a Roman Catholic to engage in depth with the Anglican tradition which is also part of my family heritage. Since then I continue to teach George Herbert to graduate students on both sides of the Atlantic. My background as a historian and theologian means that I approach the texts in a particular way. However, I am also grateful for insights over the years from colleagues who are English literature scholars.

Apart from successive classes of graduate students, I am particularly grateful to a number of people. First of all, Bishop Mark Santer began the process by initially lending me his copy of Herbert's poetry. Second, fellow staff and the ordinands at Westcott House taught me an immense amount about the riches of the Anglican tradition and what it means to live within it. The immediate result was a short book on the spirituality of Herbert which is no longer in print. In terms of the present book, I am grateful to Christine Smith at SCM-Canterbury Press for encouraging me to contribute a volume on George Herbert to the Canterbury Press series of Studies in spiritual theology. Finally, the endowment for The Joseph Visiting Professorship enabled me to spend a year at Boston College, Massachusetts, where colleagues in the Theology Department and in the School of Theology & Ministry provided a warm and supportive environment while I completed the book.

In common with modern editions of George Herbert, I have used in this book the 1652 first edition of *The Country Parson* and the 1633 first edition of *The Temple*. The most accessible editions of the complete texts of both these works are noted in the Further Reading section, page 172. In addition, Herbert's letters and Walton's *Life* appear in the Pasternak

Slater edition. Readers will notice that two poems, 'Discipline' and 'Prayer (2)', appear twice because they are so apposite in their contexts.

As always, I owe a special debt to Susie who originally persuaded me to turn my enthusiasm for George Herbert into a book. I dedicate this new Study in Herbert to her with love and gratitude.

Philip Sheldrake
Boston College
2009

Introduction

George Herbert and the Seventeenth-Century Church

George Herbert (1593–1633) was a complex person who led a varied life before he finally settled down as a country parish priest for a short period prior to his death. This very complexity, and the inner tensions that it undoubtedly produced, resulted in some memorable writing and a rich spirituality. The chapters that follow attempt to sketch some of the themes that stand out as most important: Herbert's deep biblical and liturgical roots; his Christ-centred spirituality; his emphasis on the importance of the everyday; his strong sense of place; his understanding of discipleship; his approach to prayer and, finally, his spirituality of service.

Nowadays, Herbert is considered one the greatest English poets as well as a significant, if less imaginative, writer of prose. Two of his works have achieved a special status and this volume concentrates on these. The first is the collection of poems known as *The Temple* and the other is his treatise on the life of a priest, entitled *The Country Parson*.

The writings of George Herbert also mark him out as one of the major figures in the emergence of a distinctive 'Anglican' spirituality during the seventeenth century. Of course, neither Herbert nor his contemporaries would have used the word 'Anglican' to describe the Church of England to which they belonged and its traditions. The current usage of the terms Anglican and Anglicanism seems to be a nineteenth-century invention.[1]

---

1 For more detailed studies of spirituality in the Anglican tradition, see G. Rowell, K. Stephenson and R. Williams, eds., *Love's Redeeming Work: The Anglican Quest for Holiness*, Oxford: Oxford University Press, 2001; W. Countryman, *The Poetic Imagination: An Anglican Spiritual Tradition*, London: Darton Longman and Todd/New York: Orbis Books, 1999; A. Bartlett, *A Passionate Balance: The Anglican Tradition*, London: Darton Longman and Todd/New York: Orbis Books, 2007.

Herbert was a friend of other important religious figures of the period such as Bishop Lancelot Andrewes and Nicholas Ferrar, the founder of the Little Gidding community, to whom Herbert bequeathed his writings. Several of Herbert's poems have become well-known hymns that have achieved ecumenical popularity. The profundity of the poetry also inspired the great twentieth-century English composer Ralph Vaughan Williams to set several poems to music as *The Five Mystical Songs*. To some people Herbert is an uncanonized saint, perhaps even a mystic. His impact spans the centuries. Several of his poems appear in the alternative readings in the Roman Catholic Divine Office. They even influenced such a religiously unconventional figure as Simone Weil. Just before the Second World War, Weil spent Easter at the abbey of Solesmes where she was introduced to Herbert's poetry by a young English visitor. As with so many other people, the poem known as 'Love (3)' had a special impact on her. Simone Weil used it regularly for meditation and the poem seems to have been the medium for a powerful mystical experience of the presence of Christ. George Herbert's spiritual influence as well as literary reputation lives on and his burial place in front of the altar at Bemerton village church, just outside Salisbury, still attracts visitors.

George Herbert's Life

Before we reflect on George Herbert's writings and spirituality, it is important to understand something of his context. This context implies both Herbert's own background and life as well as the situation of the Church of England in the early part of the seventeenth century.

George Herbert was born in 1593 into the aristocratic and powerful Pembroke family. He had an illustrious academic record as a pupil at Westminster School and then at Trinity College, Cambridge where he suffered regular ill health as can be seen in a letter to his step-father, Sir John Danvers, but eventually became a Fellow in 1614. Herbert seemed destined for a significant academic and public career. He became Public Orator of the University in 1620, described in another letter to Sir John Danvers, and then Member of Parliament for Monmouth (1624). The reasons why Herbert changed his course and settled on ordination may be guessed at but are not available to us in any explicit way.

George Herbert appears to have begun the study of Divinity as early as 1616. Yet he chose to be ordained as a deacon only in the aftermath of the 1624 Parliament. At that point his ordination was hastily arranged with a special dispensation from the Archbishop of Canterbury. Once again the expected pattern was delayed. By 1626 Herbert had been made a (non-resident) prebend of Lincoln Cathedral and given the living of Leighton Bromswold in Huntingdonshire near to the community of his friend, Nicholas Ferrar, who later helped Herbert with the care of the church and parish (see the letter of March 1631). However, Herbert was not ordained priest until September 1630, by which time he had already taken up residence with his family (his wife and three adopted daughters of a deceased sister) as Rector of the villages of Fugglestone and Bemerton just outside Salisbury. Unlike many aristocratic clergy, Herbert actually chose to live in the Bemerton rectory alongside his parishioners and next to the smaller and less distinguished of the two churches. His ministry as parish priest lasted less than three years for he died on 1 March 1633. During his brief ministry he appears to have concentrated his energies on the daily round of worship and on pastoral care.

The various delays in Herbert's life pattern make it reasonable to suppose that he went through a period of struggle during 1616–24 and perhaps again after ordination as a deacon. It is possible to hazard a reasonable guess at the causes. First of all it is likely that he was influenced by important external events. I have said that Herbert seems to have had ambitions of a public career. We need to leave behind the image of Herbert as simply a quiet, saintly and humble priest as portrayed in Isaak Walton's life. In reality he had close connections by blood or marriage with several of the most powerful families of the land. It is clear from his writings that Herbert continued to have a highly developed sense of civic community and public duty. This was expressed in loyalty to the local village, the wider Church and to the commonwealth of the nation. Several references in *The Country Parson* underline this concern. 'His children he [the parish priest] first makes Christians, and then commonwealth's men' (Chapter X). The priest is 'to do his country true and laudable service when occasion requires' (Chapter XIX).

The suddenness with which Herbert moved to ordination as deacon in 1624 suggests that there was some connection between his decision and what had taken place in parliament during his time as a Member of Parliament. King James I had gained a great deal of support for his attractive image of England as a peaceful country set apart from the almost perpetual religious wars on the continent. However, the failure of Prince Charles to obtain a Spanish bride, and the supposed affront this offered to the English Crown, led to increasing pressure within parliament for war with Spain. The Prince's faction appeared to have succeeded when the King dissolved the treaty of peace with Spain. This train of events, and the disappointment it produced, may well have been a factor in Herbert's decision (as well as that of his fellow Member of Parliament and close friend, Nicholas Ferrar) to turn his back on a political career.

Perhaps, in a more personal way, Herbert's struggle also concerned the contrary attractions of a public career and of vocation to the priesthood. It is not too fanciful to interpret elements of Herbert's later struggles as a consequence of the radical change of direction he had taken. Perhaps there are hints of this in one of Herbert's poems about prayer, 'Prayer (2)'. We may give up all the obvious advantages of worldly security and success yet the human relationship with God does not merely make up for the loss but actually offers more.

> I value prayer so,
>   That were I to leave all but one,
> Wealth, fame, endowments, virtues, all should go;
> I and dear prayer would together dwell,
> And quickly gain, for each inch lost, an ell.

Finally, there is much evidence in Herbert's writings to suggest that his struggle also involved a persistent sense of unworthiness in the face of God's love.

The Church of England and the Caroline Divines

The religious context for George Herbert's writings is a period shaped by a varied group of writers known as the 'Caroline Divines'. This title reflects the fact that many of these writers flourished during the reigns of Charles I and Charles II. However, the term 'Caroline' refers rather loosely to a period that began with Richard Hooker's *On the Laws of Ecclesiastical Polity* at the end of Elizabeth's reign in the late sixteenth century and concluded with William Law's *Serious Call to a Devout and Holy Life* which appeared during the reign of George I in the early eighteenth century. The period was marked by a number of critical events. First, under Charles I Archbishop Laud attempted to impose an aesthetic and ritualistic uniformity in worship. Then followed the Civil War, the Commonwealth, the apparent triumph of Puritanism and the temporary dismantling of the Church of England. The restoration of the monarchy and the Established Church in 1660 was not the end of the upheavals for the last Stuart king. James II was considered too autocratic and too Roman Catholic and was, in turn, overthrown in 1689 and replaced by William of Orange and his wife Mary. This event divided the Church of England and a number of bishops and clergy, known as Non-Jurors, resigned and went into exile.

The period was also a time of considerable religious scholarship. The work of Richard Hooker began to be assimilated into the thinking of the Church during Herbert's youth and young adulthood. Herbert's lifetime saw the true beginnings of a Church of England theology that was distinct from the strict Calvinism and Presbyterian preferences of the Puritans on the one hand and from reformed Roman Catholicism on the other. More than anything, however, the Caroline period was a time of spiritual renewal and of an increase in teaching on personal and common prayer and on the conduct of the Christian life.

As a Church of the Reformation (while not a wholly reformed Church in the minds of some critics), the Church of England was unusual in taking an interest in the spiritual development and guidance of individual Christians. The Caroline period produced a large number of writings that, in different ways, offered a pattern for Christian living. Interestingly, many of the writers were bishops. Much of the spiritual teaching was not systematic but appeared in sermons, collections of prayers and devotions and in poetry. Because the liturgy of the Church was so central to the emerging tradition, many of the writings were in practice companion volumes to the *Book of Common Prayer*. There is also some evidence for the influence in England of some post-Reformation Roman Catholic writers such as St Francis de Sales, as well as the continued availability of pre-Reformation works such as Walter Hilton's spiritual treatise *The Ladder of Perfection* and the *Imitation of Christ* reputedly by the Dutch Augustinian monk Thomas à Kempis.

Among the Caroline writers themselves there was a variety of styles. There were pastoral treatises on the Christian life such as Bishop Bayley's *The Practice of Piety*. Bishop Jeremy Taylor's *The Rule and Exercises of Holy Living* linked spirituality closely with ethics. Bishop Joseph Hall, while theologically Calvinist, drew on late medieval spirituality among other sources for his book on prayer, *The Arte of Divine Meditation*. Bishop John Cosin attempted to fill the devotional gap that seemed to be attracting some members of the royal court towards Rome. Cosin's *A Collection of Private Devotions* taught the observance of holy days, ritualized liturgy, sacramental confession and frequent communion. The value of individual confession and spiritual guidance was also touched upon in the writings of Bishop Jeremy Taylor and George Herbert. Bishop Lancelot Andrewes, a friend and mentor of Herbert, drew on a wide variety of sources, patristic and medieval, Western and Eastern, in his sermons and his cycle of prayers known as *Preces Privatae*. Cardinal Newman used this little book for his thanksgiving after daily communion until his death. Then there was the poetry and evocative prose not only of Herbert but of John Donne, Henry Vaughan and Thomas Traherne to name but a few. Interestingly, the most mystical of the writers, Herbert, Vaughan and Traherne, all had strong Welsh connections.

Spiritual Emphases

As we shall see in the first section of this volume, the Bible and the liturgy of the 1559 revision of the *Book of Common Prayer* were the two key foundations of Church of England spirituality in Herbert's time. However, there were several other important characteristics of Caroline spirituality. First, it was strongly Christ-centred. Christ was not only the privileged revelation of God and the means of God's saving action, but he was also the explicit pattern of Christian living. There was a special but not exclusive emphasis on the passion of Christ in a number of writers. In some cases this underpinned a sense that God's just anger with human sin was held at bay by Christ taking upon himself the guilty verdict delivered against humanity. There are some hints of this in Herbert but his predominant image is not of God's justice but of God's love revealed in Christ.

Other important themes were those of creation and the Incarnation. Some aspects of Calvinist doctrine were taken for granted in the Church of England. However, most Caroline writers opposed the rejection of material reality and earthly concerns that characterized both more radical Calvinists and the Roman Catholic Jansenists on the continent. Christian Humanism, inspired by such people as Erasmus, John Colet and Thomas More, had played a significant role at various stages of the English Reformation. A residual humanism was certainly present in the seventeenth century and may explain why certain continental Roman Catholic writers such as St Francis de Sales were so popular. Practical service of others was emphasized and prayer was to be focused on earthly as well as heavenly concerns. Although some of the poetry of

Herbert and Donne reminds us that this period was preoccupied with sin and death, a note of spiritual joy was very evident as well. A particular joy in God's creation characterizes some of the poetry of Henry Vaughan and the *Centuries of Meditations* of Thomas Traherne.

Catholic or Protestant?

One obvious fact that united all the spiritualities of the Reformation period, Protestant or Roman Catholic, is that they were a response to the failures of late medieval theology and devotion. In the later Middle Ages there was widespread anxiety about the worth of human effort in the quest for holiness. In many respects, the early struggles of Martin Luther prior to 1517 are a paradigm of the basic dilemma. He strove to observe the rule of his reformed Augustinian community with great rigour, had a longing to imitate the desert fathers of the early Church and tried to combat his moral scruples with frequent sacramental confession. On a subjective level, these traditional means of asceticism and religious practice failed to assuage his sense of guilt and spiritual inadequacy. More objectively, Luther came to see that even if he was theoretically capable of earning salvation by intense effort, no experience could guarantee whether he was justified or not. God demanded perfection but the problem was that it was impossible for anyone to know whether they had reached such a state or fallen short. For Luther, the result was a sense of futility and near-despair from which he was liberated by the realization of justification by faith alone. In a general sense, George Herbert accepted Luther's 'solution'.

There has been some controversy about whether Herbert's writings should be considered essentially 'Protestant' or 'Catholic'. Some scholars have emphasized Herbert's place within the predominantly 'Catholic' structures and liturgy of the Church of England, based on a traditional three-fold ministry and the Prayer Book. The evidence produced consists of the medieval allusions in Herbert's works and his undoubtedly liturgical and sacramental spirituality. The 'Catholic' school of interpretation also tends to draw attention to the influences of post-Reformation Roman Catholic spiritual writers on seventeenth-century Anglicans.

Because this interpretation was one-sided, it was inevitably corrected by 'Protestant' revisionism. This standpoint re-emphasized that the Church of England was really a Reformed Church, more Genevan than Lutheran, even if there were continuities with the medieval past.

According to this interpretation, Herbert's theology must have been unequivocally Protestant and specifically Calvinist. More recent studies have attempted to mediate between these two poles. Thus, what is implied by the terms 'Catholic' and 'Protestant' is not as mutually exclusive as was once thought. Members of the Church of England in Herbert's time, of whatever party, undoubtedly thought of themselves as Protestant. This did not mean that there was no sense of continuity with the pre-Reformation Catholic past. After all, an undoubted Puritan such as Isaac Ambrose could happily quote St Bernard of Clairvaux on the Song of Songs. The seventeenth-century Church of England had a particularity which tended to be overlooked in the past but which contemporary scholars are more inclined to acknowledge. Apologists for the Church of England believed that their Church beautifully mediated between the two extremes of Geneva and Rome. Indeed, Herbert's own poem 'The British Church' took just such a stance.[2]

In Herbert's day, there were undoubtedly strict Calvinists within the Church of England. Indeed, the religious settlement under Elizabeth I committed the Church as a whole to a Calvinist doctrine of predestination, described as 'full of sweet, pleasant and unspeakable comfort' in Article 17 of the Thirty-Nine Articles of Religion. However, the Church of England of the early seventeenth century could not be labelled simply as Calvinist. Even Article 17 is ambiguous about the stricter Calvinist doctrine of double predestination.

George Herbert seems to have been typical of most non-Puritan writers of his time in accepting aspects of Calvinist doctrine while not being a thoroughgoing Calvinist. He was a friend of other contemporary spiritual figures such as Bishop Lancelot Andrewes and Nicholas Ferrar whose theologies and spiritualities, like Herbert's own, were complex. Herbert's writings appear to argue in a simple way for loyalty to the established liturgy and doctrines of the Church of England. In the context of the times, however, this was a less eirenical and a more contentious position than appears to be the case at first glance. Herbert's church connections, not least with Ferrar, his involvement in restoring and beautifying church buildings, as well as his defence of priestly

---

2 For one classic 'Catholic' interpretation, see R. Tuve, *A Reading of George Herbert*, Chicago: University of Chicago Press [1952], reprint 1982. For an example of 'Protestant' revisionism, see B. Lewalski, *Protestant Poetics and the Seventeenth-Century Religious Lyric*, Princeton: Princeton University Press, 1979. For the mediating 'Anglican' interpretation see S. Sykes, *Unashamed Anglicanism*, London: Darton Longman and Todd, 1999, Chapter 3, 'Love bade me welcome'.

blessings, confession, processions, the use of the sign of the cross and, obliquely, of liturgical dress may be interpreted as a counter-blast to Puritanism. There is also some evidence in Herbert's poetic collection *The Temple* of a tension between the classical Reformed doctrines of predestination and justification by faith and a sense of human freedom and responsibility. Herbert clearly believed that the Church to which he gave his loyalty made it possible to hold together the Reformation doctrines of grace, redemption and faith with a continued stress on the centrality of liturgy, the value of a sacramental life and the need for personal holiness. Thus, debates about Herbert's 'Protestantism' or 'Catholicism' cannot be resolved in a simple way in one direction rather than another and are in that sense unhelpful.

There is one specific question to address. Was Herbert's spirituality, like that of some of his contemporaries, influenced by contemporary Roman Catholicism? Because the Church of England retained substantial continuities with its Catholic past it was certainly susceptible to influences from continental spirituality. For example, Ignatian spirituality, sometimes in mediated forms (for example through the writings of St Francis de Sales), had a discernible impact on some seventeenth-century Anglicans. The degree to which Ignatian approaches to prayer or the spiritual life directly influenced specific figures such as George Herbert has been the subject of some argument in recent years. In contrast to the writings of the former Roman Catholic John Donne where there are obvious echoes of Ignatian approaches, there do not seem to be discernible connections between Herbert and Ignatius Loyola. In Herbert's long poem 'Perirrhanterium' (lines 451–6) in the opening section of *The Temple*, there is a probable allusion to the devotional practice of a daily examination of conscience that is so characteristic of Ignatian spirituality. Yet this does not prove a great deal because similar devotional exercises had become widespread by the early seventeenth century. At most Herbert may, like others of his contemporaries, have been aware in a general way of elements of Catholic Reformation spirituality, but it seems unlikely that these played a significant role in his writings.

Writings: Purpose and Audience

The dating of George Herbert's two great works, the poetic collection *The Temple* and the prose treatise *The Country Parson*, as well as their precise purpose, are also matters of debate. Even their titles are contentious. There are three major texts of the poetry. It seems that Herbert's preferred title was *The Church* (as in manuscript W which has corrections in Herbert's own hand) and that this was subsequently changed to *The Temple* in a later revised and expanded manuscript B from which the first printed edition of 1633 derives. Both works were published after Herbert's death – the poems in 1633 with a preface by his friend Nicholas Ferrar and the prose treatise as late as 1652 when Herbert's probable title *The Country Parson* was changed to the rather grander *A Priest to the Temple*.[3] It used to be thought that Herbert wrote both works while parish priest at Bemerton. It is now widely accepted that, while Herbert probably edited and structured the works there, he wrote a significant number of the poems before 1630. As far as *The Country Parson* is concerned, his remarks in the 1632 preface, 'I have resolved to set down the form and character of a true pastor, that I may have a mark to aim at,' suggest that the work was written in anticipation of taking up parochial ministry. There is certainly no real indication that the text is a description of his personal experiences at Bemerton.

Even if the main arguments of *The Country Parson* were largely complete prior to active ministry in Bemerton, the preface is nevertheless dated 1632. This suggests that Herbert did not feel it necessary to change the overall content or tone while he was a parish priest. It also makes it likely that Herbert had a didactic purpose even if present-day readers may feel that his portrait of a parish priest was somewhat idealized. The most obvious conclusion to draw from the preface is that the work was intended to offer a model for others rather than simply to be a private expression of Herbert's own sense of duty. The concluding sentence of the preface runs 'The Lord prosper the intention to myself and others, who may not despise my poor labours, but add to those points which I have observed, until the book grow to a complete pastoral.' In the context, 'the others' would most likely be fellow ministers or those considering such a calling.

Is the work essentially a description of the priest's duties and a manual for the communication of practical information? Such an approach is too simple. Modern commentators on Herbert's works emphasize the rhetorical style of his surrounding culture and how this shows it-

---

3 On manuscript questions, see the Introduction to Ann Pasternak Slater, ed., *George Herbert: The Complete English Works*, Everyman's Library 204, London: David Campbell Publishers, revised edition 1995.

self specifically in *The Country Parson* and *The Temple*. The rhetorical style probably originates in the tradition of Renaissance humanism that certainly influenced Herbert and his circle. However, such a style also represented a return to the Bible (especially St Paul) and to the theology of the early Christian era (especially St Augustine). Rhetoric sought to communicate much more than information or argument. Its purpose was evoke love, feelings and imagination and thus to move the human heart to a response.

The prose treatise is a work of rhetoric in two senses. This style was actually intended to move the writing beyond the pedantic and gives it spiritual depth even though, to contemporary taste, the work feels remarkably detached. In the first place the book is meant not simply to *instruct* but to *move* the reader to a deepening sense of call. In the second place the text portrays the priest as a rhetorician. That is, his fundamental task, in what he says, does and lives, is to move his parishioners to deeper faith and to greater involvement in the life of the Christian community.

The poems are also a work of rhetoric. Isaak Walton, the seventeenth-century author of Herbert's life, attributes a message from him to Nicholas Ferrar concerning the collection of poems known as *The Temple*. They are 'a picture of the many spiritual conflicts that have passed betwixt God and my soul before I could subject mine to the will of Jesus my Master; in which service I have now found perfect freedom'. Even if the personal tone of these words is authentic Herbert, it is widely agreed that *The Temple*, published in 1633 shortly after Herbert's death, also has a conscious structure as a work of religious teaching. In that sense, it appears that the poems are equally as pastoral as *The Country Parson*. While many of the poems are almost certainly genuine expressions of Herbert's own experience, their purpose is not essentially autobiographical in our modern sense. That is to say that, as with St Augustine's *Confessions*, the author's purpose was not to write essentially *about* himself. For Herbert, as for St Augustine, personal experience or the self is simply a rhetorical source by means of which *God* could be communicated to the reader who would then be led to greater praise and to a deeper response.

The poems of *The Temple* are structured into a conscious movement or dynamic. Some scholars explain this in reference to certain assumptions about Herbert's theology. For example the 164 poems can be seen as a representation of the Christian pilgrimage from 'imputed righteousness' (justification) to personal holiness (sanctification), which is achieved finally only after this life. There can be little doubt that in the context of Herbert's time he accepted the classic Protestant understanding of justification by faith. However, the poems are too rich to reduce the complexity of the spiritual struggle expressed in them to a simple or single theological structure.

The scheme of the poems is closely ordered. They are gathered into a three-part structure, 'The Church Porch', 'The Church' and 'The Church Militant', of which the middle part is by far the largest. This central collection is also spiritually the richest and the most dynamic. The titles of the three sections correspond to the three different meanings of 'Temple' or 'Church'. First of all, it is a physical building, an architectural space within which God is somehow present and is praised in the liturgy. Some poems employ features of the building as a framework for their teaching; for example, 'The Altar', 'The Church-floor', 'The Windows', 'Church-monuments'. In doing this, the poems subtly underline the importance of order and beauty in the Christian life. The 'Temple' is secondly the Body of Christ, the Christian community. Thus other poems express the Church's year or liturgical order through which the community expresses and solidifies its identity; for example, 'Even-song', 'Mattins', 'Lent', 'Holy Communion'. Finally, the 'Temple' is the individual human soul, described in St Paul as the 'temple of the Holy Spirit' (1 Corinthians 3.16).

This last emphasis on the individual human person points to an important aspect of Herbert's teaching. *The Temple* is clearly meant to communicate to readers something of the Christian spiritual path. Interestingly, it seems that after Herbert's death the poems were put to a variety of instructional uses as spiritual reading alongside the Bible and the official collections of sermons, or as a source of quotations for sermons. Having said this, the poems are not primarily instructional. It is true that there is something fairly didactic and morally exhortative about 'The Church Porch', the first of the three sections of *The Temple*. However, this is not typical of the famous lyrical poems in the extensive central section, 'The Church'. Stylistically, most of the poems are addressed to God and therefore take the form of meditation or intimate conversation. Again, a rhetorical explanation seems appropriate. The poems teach by moving the reader to an affective response and therefore ultimately to a change of life. Precisely because the poems lay bare Herbert's own spiritual life for the sake of other people, they also appear to identify with the problems and aspirations of all Christians. This contrasts with the rather more detached and objective style of *The Country Parson*.

Overall, it would not be valid to describe Herbert's approach to spirituality as didactic in a narrow and pedantic sense. Even if Herbert's prose work is rather assertive and detached, this needs to be read alongside the poetry where the painful realities of inward spiritual struggle haunt the pages. Although *The Country Parson* deserves to be redeemed as a work of spiritual literature, there can be no doubt that it is the poems that make the greater spiritual as well as aesthetic impact on the modern reader.

Readings

1 Izaak Walton, *The Life of Mr George Herbert*, pp. 360–2

2 *The Country Parson*, Preface

3 *The Country Parson*, Chapter I

4 The Odour

5 The Pearl

6 Letter to Sir John Danvers, March 1617, concerning ill health

7 Letter to Sir John Danvers, September 1619, concerning his appointment as University Orator

8 Letter to his brother, Henry Herbert, Autumn 1630, concerning the care of his orphaned niece

9 Letter to Nicholas Ferrar, March 1631, concerning Leighton church

I

The Life of Mr George Herbert

IZAAK WALTON

I have now brought him to the parsonage of Bemerton, and to the thirty-sixth year of his age, and must stop here, and bespeak the reader to prepare for an almost incredible story of the great sanctity of the short remainder of his holy life; a life so full of charity, humility, and all Christian virtues, that it deserves the eloquence of St. Chrysostom to commend and declare it; a life, that if it were related by a pen like his, there would then be no need for this age to look back into times past for the examples of primitive piety, for they might be all found in the life of George Herbert. But now, alas! who is fit to undertake it? I confess I am not; and am not pleased with myself that I must; and profess myself amazed when I consider how few of the clergy lived like him then, and how many live so unlike him now. But it becomes not me to censure. My design is rather to assure the reader that I have used very great diligence to inform myself, that I might inform him of the truth of what follows; and though I cannot adorn it with eloquence, yet I will do it with sincerity.

When at his induction he was shut into Bemerton Church, being left there alone to toll the bell (as the law requires him),[4] he stayed so much longer than an ordinary time before he returned to those friends that stayed expecting him at the church door, that his friend Mr. Woodnot looked in at the church window, and saw him lie prostrate on the ground before the altar; at which time and place (as he after told Mr. Woodnot) he set some rules to himself for the future manage of his life, and then and there made a vow to labour to keep them.

And the same night that he had his induction, he said to Mr. Woodnot, 'I now look back upon my aspiring thoughts, and think myself more happy than if I had attained what then I so ambitiously thirsted for; and I can now behold the Court with an impartial eye, and see plainly that it is made up for fraud, and titles, and flattery, and many other such empty, imaginary, painted pleasures – pleasures that are so empty as not to satisfy when they are enjoyed. But in God and his service is a fulness of all joy and pleasure, and no satiety. And I will now use all my endeavours to bring my relations and dependants to a love and reliance on him, who never fails those that trust him. But, above all, I will be sure to live well, because the virtuous life of a clergyman is the most powerful eloquence to persuade all that see it to reverence and love, and at least to desire to live like him. And this I will do, because I know we live in an age that hath more need of good examples than precepts. And I beseech that God, who hath honoured me so much as to call me to serve him at his altar, that as by his special grace he hath put into my heart these good desires and resolutions; so he will, by his assisting grace, give me ghostly strength to bring the same to good effect. And I beseech him that my humble and charitable life may so win upon

---

4 To make his induction known to the parishioners.

others as to bring glory to my Jesus, whom I have this day taken to be my Master and Governor; and I am so proud of his service, that I will always observe, and obey, and do his will, and always call him Jesus, my Master; and I will always contemn my birth, or any title or dignity that can be conferred upon me, when I shall compare them with my title of being a priest, and serving at the altar of Jesus my Master.'

And that he did so may appear in many parts of his Book of *Sacred Poems*, especially in that which he calls 'The Odour' – in which he seems to rejoice in the thoughts of that word, Jesus, and say, that the adding these, my Master, to it, and the often repetition of them, seemed to perfume his mind and leave an Oriental fragrancy in his very breath. And for his unforced choice to serve at God's altar, he seems in another place of his poems, 'The Pearl,' (*Matt.* 13: 45, 46) to rejoice, and say, 'he knew the ways of learning; knew what nature does willingly, and what, when it is forced by fire; knew the ways of honour, and when glory inclines the soul to noble expressions; knew the Court; knew the ways of pleasure, of love, of wit, of music, and upon what terms he declined all these for the service of his Master Jesus'; and then concludes, saying,

That through these labyrinths, not my grovelling wit,
But thy silk twist, let down from heaven to me,
Did both conduct and teach me, how by it
    To climb to thee.

2

The Country Parson, Preface

The Author to the Reader

Being desirous (through the mercy of God) to please him, for whom I am and live, and who giveth me my desires and performances; and considering with myself that the way to please him is to feed my flock diligently and faithfully, since our Saviour hath made that the argument of a pastor's love, I have resolved to set down the form and character of a true pastor, that I may have a mark to aim at, which also I will set as high as I can, since he shoots higher that threatens the moon, than he that aims at a tree. Not that I think, if a man do not all which is here expressed, he presently sins and displeases God; but that it is a good strife to go as far as we can in pleasing of him who hath done so much for us. The Lord prosper the intention to myself and others, who may not despise my poor labours, but add to those points which I have observed, until the book grow to a complete pastoral.

3

The Country Parson, Chapter I
Of a Pastor

A Pastor is the deputy of Christ, for the reducing of man to the obedience of God. This definition is evident, and contains the direct steps of pastoral duty and authority. For, first, man fell from God by disobedience; secondly, Christ is the glorious instrument of God for the revoking of man; thirdly, Christ being not to continue on earth, but after he had fulfilled the work of reconciliation, to be received up into heaven, he constituted deputies in his place, and these are priests. And therefore St. Paul, in the beginning of his Epistles, professeth this; and in the First to the Colossians[5] plainly avoucheth that he *fills up that which is behind of the afflictions of Christ in his flesh, for his body's sake, which is the Church*,[6] wherein is contained the complete definition of a minister. Out of this charter of the priesthood may be plainly gathered both the dignity thereof and the duty: the dignity, in that a priest may do that which Christ did, and by his authority and as his vicegerent; the duty, in that a priest is to do that which Christ did, and after his manner, both for doctrine and life.

4

The Odour

How sweetly doth *My Master* sound! *My Master!*
    As Amber-grease leaves a rich scent
      Unto the taster:
    So do these words a sweet content,
An oriental fragrancy, *My Master.*

---

5 1 Colossians 1.24.

6 The first edition uses italics for quotations and, apparently, for emphasis. They may also indicate authorial afterthoughts.

With these all day I do perfume my mind,
  My mind ev'n thrust into them both:
    That I might find
  What cordials make this curious broth,
This broth of smells, that feeds and fats my mind.

My Master, shall I speak? O that to thee
  My servant were a little so,
    As flesh may be;
  That these two words might creep and grow
To some degree of spiciness to thee!

Then should the Pomander, which was before
  A speaking sweet, mend by reflection,
    And tell me more:
  For pardon of my imperfection
Would warm and work it sweeter than before.

For when *My Master*, which alone is sweet,
  And ev'n in my unworthiness pleasing,
    Shall call and meet,
  My servant, as thee not displeasing,
That call is but the breathing of the sweet.

This breathing would with gains by sweetning me
  (As sweet things traffic when they meet)
    Return to thee.
  And so this new commerce and sweet
Should all my life employ, and busy me.

5

The Pearl

I know the ways of learning; both the head
And pipes that feed the press, and make it run;
What reason hath from nature borrowed,
Or of it self, like a good housewife, spun
In laws and policy; what the stars conspire,
What willing nature speaks, what forc'd by fire;

Both th' old discoveries, and the new-found seas,
The stock and surplus, cause and history:
All these stand open, or I have the keys:
    Yet I love thee.

I know the ways of honour, what maintains
The quick returns of courtesy and wit:
In vies of favours whether party gains,
When glory swells the heart, and mouldeth it
To all expressions both of hand and eye,
Which on the world a true-love-knot may tie,
And bear the bundle, wheresoe're it goes:
How many drams of spirit there must be
To sell my life unto my friends or foes:
    Yet I love thee.

I know the ways of pleasure, the sweet strains,
The lullings and the relishes of it;
The propositions of hot blood and brains;
What mirth and music mean; what love and wit
Have done these twenty hundred years, and more:
I know the projects of unbridled store:
My stuff is flesh, not brass; my senses live,
And grumble oft, that they have more in me
Then he that curbs them, being but one to five:
    Yet I love thee.

I know all these, and have them in my hand:
Therefore not seeled, but with open eyes
I fly to thee, and fully understand
Both the main sale, and the commodities;
And at what rate and price I have thy love;
With all the circumstances that may move:
Yet through the labyrinths, not my grovelling wit,
But thy silk twist let down from heav'n to me,
Did both conduct and teach me, how by it
    To climb to thee.

6

Letter to Sir John Danvers, March 1617

Sir,

I dare no longer be silent, lest while I think I am modest, I wrong both my self, and also the confidence my Friends have in me; wherefore I will open my case unto you, which I think deserves the reading at the least; and it is this. I want books extremely. You know Sir, how I am now setting foot into Divinity, to lay the platform of my future life, and shall I then be fain always to borrow books, and build on another's foundation? What tradesman is there who will set up without his tools? Pardon my boldness Sir, it is a most serious case, nor can I write coldly in that, wherein consisteth the making good of my former education, of obeying that spirit which hath guided me hitherto, and of achieving my (I dare say) holy ends. This also is aggravated, in that I apprehend what my friends would have been forward to say, if I had taken ill courses, *Follow your book, and you shall want nothing.* You know Sir, it is their ordinary speech, and now let them make it good; for since I hope I have not deceived their expectation, let not them deceive mine. But perhaps they will say, you are sickly, you must not study too hard. It is true (God knows) I am weak, yet not so, but that every day, I may step one step towards my journey's end; and I love my friends so well, as that if all things proved not well, I had rather the fault should lie on me than on them. But they will object again, What becomes of your annuity? Sir, if there be any truth in me, I find it little enough to keep me in health. You know I was sick last vacation, neither am I yet recovered, so that I am fain ever and anon, to buy somewhat tending towards my health; for infirmities are both painful and costly. Now this Lent I am forbid utterly to eat any Fish, so that I am fain to diet in my Chamber at mine own cost; for in our public Halls, you know, is nothing but fish and Whit-meats. Out of Lent also, twice a week, on Fridays and Saturdays, I must do so, which yet sometimes I fast. Sometimes, also I ride to Newmarket and there lie a day or two for fresh air; all which tend to avoiding of costlier matters, if I should fall absolutely sick. I protest and vow, I even study thrift, and yet I am scarce able with much ado to make one half year's allowance shake hands with the other. And yet if a book of four or five shillings come in my way, I buy it, though I fast for it; yea, sometimes of ten shillings. But, alas Sir, what is that to those infinite volumes of divinity, which yet every day swell, and grow bigger. Noble Sir, pardon my boldness, and consider but these three things. First, the bulk of divinity. Secondly, the time when I desire this (which is now, when I must lay the foundation of my whole life). Thirdly, what I desire, and to what end, not vain pleasures, nor to a vain end. If then, Sir, there be any course, either by engaging my future annuity, or any other way, I desire you, Sir, to be my mediator to them in my behalf.

Now I write to you, Sir, because to you I have ever opened my heart; and have reason, by the patents of your perpetual favour to do so still, for I am sure you love

Your faithfullest Servant,
George Herbert

7

Letter to Sir John Danvers, September 1619

Sir,

This Week hath loaded me with your favours; I wish I could have come in person to thank you, but it is not possible. Presently after Michaelmas, I am to make an Oration to the whole University of an hour long in Latin, and my Lincoln journey hath set me much behind hand: neither can I so much as go to Bugden, and deliver your letter, yet have I sent it thither by a faithful messenger this day. I beseech you all, you and my dear mother and sister to pardon me, for my Cambridge necessities are stronger to tie me here, than yours to London. If I could possibly have come, none should have done my message to Sir Francis Nethersole for me; he and I are ancient acquaintance, and I have a strong opinion of him, that if he can do me a courtesy, he will of himself; yet your appearing in it, affects me strangely. I have sent you here enclosed a letter from our master in my behalf, which if you can send to Sir Francis before his departure, it will do well, for it expresseth the University's inclination to me; yet if you cannot send it with much convenience, it is no matter, for the gentleman needs no incitation to love me.

The orator's place (that you may understand what it is) is the finest place in the University, though not the gainfullest; yet that will be about 30 *l. per an.* but the commodiousness is beyond the revenue; for the orator writes all the university letters, makes all the orations, be it to King, prince, or whatever comes to the university; to requite these pains, he takes place next the doctors, is at all their assemblies and meetings, and sits above the proctors, is regent or non-regent at his pleasure, and such like gaynesses, which will please a young man well.

I long to hear from Sir Francis; I pray Sir send the letter you receive from him to me as soon as you can, that I may work the heads to my purpose. I hope I shall get this place without all your London helps, of which I am very proud, not but that I joy in your favours, but that you may see, that if all fail, yet I am able to stand on mine own legs. Noble Sir, I thank you for your infinite favours, I fear only that I have omitted some fitting circumstance, yet you will pardon my haste, which is very great, though never so, but that I have both time and work to be

Your extreme Servant,
George Herbert.

8

Letter to his brother, Henry Herbert, Autumn 1630

Dear Bro;

That you did not only entertain my proposals, but advance them, was lovingly done, and like a good brother. Yet truly it was none of my meaning, when I wrote, to put one of our nieces into your hands but barely what I wrote I meant, and no more; and am glad that although you offer more, yet you will do as you write, that also. I was desirous to put a good mind into the way of charity, and that was all I intended. For concerning your offer of receiving one, I will tell you what I wrote to our eldest brother, when he urged one upon me, and but one, and that at my choice. I wrote to him that I would have both or neither; and that upon this ground, because they were to come into an unknown country, tender in knowledge, sense, and age, and knew none but one who could be no company to them. Therefore I considered that if one only came, the comfort intended would prove a discomfort. Since that I have seen the fruit of my observation, for they have lived so lovingly, lying, eating, walking, praying, working, still together, that I take a comfort therein; and would not have to part them yet, till I take some opportunity to let them know your love, for which both they shall, and I do, thank you. It is true there is a third sister, whom to receive were the greatest charity of all, for she is youngest, and least looked unto; having none to do it but her school-mistress, and you know what those mercenary creatures are. Neither hath she any to repair unto at good times, as Christmas, etc. which, you know, is the encouragement of learning all the year after, except my cousin Bett take pity of her, which yet at that distance is some difficulty. If you could think of taking her, as once you did, surely it were a great good deed, and I would have her conveyed to you. But I judge you not: do that which God shall put into your heart, and the Lord bless all your purposes to his glory. Yet, truly if you take her not, I am thinking to do it, even beyond my strength; especially at this time, being more beggarly now than I have been these many years, as having spent two hundred pounds in building; which to me that have nothing yet, is very much. But though I both consider this, and your observation also of the unthankfulness of kindred bred up (which generally is very true) yet I care not; I forget all things, so I may do them good who want it. So I do my part to them, let them think of me what they will or can. I have another judge, to whom I stand or fall. If I should regard such things, it were in another's power to defeat my charity, and evil should be stronger than good: but difficulties are so far from cooling christians, that they whet them. Truly it grieves me to think of the child, how destitute she is, and that in this necessary time of education. For the time of breeding is the time of doing children good; and not as many who think they have done fairly, if they leave them a good portion after their decease. But take this rule, and it is an outlandish one, which I commend to you as being now a father, 'the best-bred child hath the best portion'. Well; the good God bless you more and more; and all yours; and make your family a household of God's servants. So prays

Your ever loving brother,
G. Herbert

9

Letter to Nicholas Ferrar, March 1631

My exceeding Dear Brother.

    Although you have a much better Paymaster than myself, even him, whom we both serve: yet I shall ever put your care of Leighton upon my account, and give you myself for it, to be yours for ever. God knows, I have desired a long time to do the place good, and have endeavoured many ways, to find out a man for it. And now my gracious Lord God is pleased to give me you for the man I desired, for which I humbly thank him, and am so far from giving you cause to apology about your counselling me herein, that I take it exceeding kindly of you. I refuse not advice from the meanest that creeps upon God's earth, no not tho' the advice step so far, as to be reproof: much less can I disesteem it from you, whom I esteem to be God's faithful and diligent servant, not considering you any other ways, as neither I my self desire to be considered. Particularly, I like all your Addresses, and for aught I see, they are ever to be liked. [*So he goes on in the discourse of the building of the Church, in such & such a form as N.F. advised, & letting N.F. know, all he had, & would do, to get moneys to proceed in it. And concludes thus.*] You write very lovingly that all your things are mine. If so, let this of Leighton Church the care be amongst the chiefest also, so also have I required Mr W. for his part. Now God the Father of our Lord Jesus Christ bless you more and more, and so turn you all, in your several ways, one to the other, that ye may be a heavenly comfort, to his praise and the great joy of

Your brother and Servant in Christ Jesus

George Herbert

Bible and Liturgy

The foundations of George Herbert's spirituality are firmly rooted in the context of seventeenth-century English social and religious values and structures. Although the notion of spirituality these days tends to be highly personal, if not individualistic, Herbert's vision was quite different. For him, to be human implied that people belonged to a community that was both social (the nation or state) and spiritual (the Church). One of the most striking characteristics of Herbert's spirituality is that it is completely rooted in the life of the Church. In turn, the life of the church community was founded on two equal elements: the Bible and common worship or liturgy.

The Bible

As a Church of the Reformation, the Church of England set great store on the Bible. Two of the Thirty-Nine Articles of Religion (numbers VI & VII) refer directly to the role of Scripture and accept the fundamental Reformation principle that 'Holy Scripture containeth all things necessary to salvation'. This emphasis on Scripture had a practical impact on the lives and spirituality of Christians through the greater availability of vernacular Bibles and even more generally through the new liturgy. Thomas Cranmer's reform of the English liturgy in itself exposed worshippers to a greater amount of Scripture (and in English) than had previously been the case. This was particularly true because Cranmer made the daily Offices accessible to lay people rather than limited to clergy or to members of religious orders by reducing their number and simplifying their structure. According to the rubrics for the Offices of Mattins and Evensong, the whole of the Psalter was recited over a month. At the same time, the whole Bible was to be read in the course of a year by means of two substantial readings at every Office; one from the Old Testament and the other from the New Testament. In addition, of course, there were the biblical readings at celebrations of the Holy Communion. On Sundays and Festivals, the reading of Scripture was to be supported by preaching.

Throughout his writings, Herbert shows himself to be a devoted servant of Scripture. In his *The Country Parson* he suggests that at the very heart of the parson's life and ministry lie the sacred Scriptures. These are a primary means of divine inspiration and of spiritual transformation, both in the priest's own life and as an instrument of evangelization. Almost every aspect of Herbert's poetry can be traced directly or indirectly to the Bible. The directness of biblical language and the pointedness of biblical allusion suited Herbert's desire for lucidity rather than artifice in his verse. As for example in the poem 'The Holy Scriptures (2)', he drew freely on the overall atmosphere of Scripture, as well as on specific biblical allusions or references, to lay bare the inner world of human experience and particularly the struggle between God and the turbulent emotions of the human heart. For this reason, Herbert sets a high store on the priest's engagement with Scripture as the fundamental source for life and ministry (*The Country Parson*, Chapter IV). It is reasonable to suggest that, in the context of the times, this reflected the 'reformed' sensibilities of the Church of England. At the heart of the parson's knowledge and ministry lie the sacred Scriptures. Herbert believed in the power and potential of preaching and that preaching was fundamentally an exposition of the Scriptures (*The Country Parson*, Chapter VII).

A number of scholars have drawn a quite sharp distinction between Protestant and Catholic styles of meditative engagement with Scripture in Herbert's time. One important element is the relationship between the texts of Scripture (particularly those such as the Psalms that highlight deep emotions) and individual human lives. It has been suggested that the spirituality of the Catholic Reformation was far less concerned with inner emotions, particularly troublesome ones, than Protestant styles of meditation. Thus, Herbert's way of relating the Bible to the inner world of his experience, and his portrayal of God dwelling in the human heart, have been contrasted with the approach of Francis de Sales whose works were well known in England in Herbert's time. On this score, Herbert's meditative sensibilities in relation to Scripture were classically Protestant. While this statement may well be true, an over-polarized distinction between Protestant and Catholic meditative approaches may be too sharply drawn. To relate the words of Scripture to personal experience and particularly to inner emotional struggles is as characteristic in its own way of Ignatius Loyola in his *Spiritual Exercises* as it is of George Herbert.

Among the biblical books, Herbert was apparently particularly fond of the Wisdom literature, the Book of Psalms and the parables in the Gospels. Within the Wisdom books, Herbert's favourite appears to be the Book of Proverbs. This is reflected not only in the production of Herbert's own collection of over a thousand proverbs, *Outlandish Proverbs*, but also in the echoes of the biblical proverbs in the over-lengthy and rather didactic poem 'Perirrhanterium' in the first section of the *Temple* poems, 'The Church Porch'. Having said this, the poem does contain some good advice about practical behaviour and morals in the style of the biblical book. A number of the later poems of *The Temple*, for example, 'Redemption', echo the style of the Gospel parables. Indeed, echoes of a parable style may be detected in all of Herbert's poems that involve any kind of narrative. The effect, as in the parables of the Gospels, is to teach by means of an indirect discourse. This is both a means of engaging the audience with serious issues through the immediacy of narrative and, at the same time, of teasing the audience to think and imagine their way beyond the immediate story to the moral or spiritual point.

It is generally agreed that the single greatest biblical influence and allusion throughout the poems of *The Temple* is the Book of Psalms. Although Herbert actually wrote only one poetic version of a psalm, 'The 23 Psalm', more general echoes of the Psalter reverberate throughout his poetry. Another poem, 'Discipline', is effectively a restructuring of Psalm 38. This was one of the seven so-called Penitential Psalms that seem to have had a particular attraction for Herbert. George Herbert was especially impressed by the devotional nature of the Psalms. They were obviously suitable for Herbert's purposes as their wide emotional range illustrated the complexities and struggles of the human heart. The Psalms seem to have been part of Herbert's life in a number of ways. A relative of his, Sir Philip Sidney, had made his own translation of the psalms. The daily recitation of the whole Psalter was a central discipline of the Little Gidding community led by Herbert's great friend and spiritual confidant, Nicholas Ferrar. The greatest influence of all, of course, was the liturgy of the Church of England where the two-fold daily Office, of which Herbert was so fond, exposed him to a regular cycle of psalms. Interestingly, Herbert's references are consistently to the translation of the Psalms in the Great Bible of 1539 which was the version used in the liturgy and eventually formally incorporated into the Prayer Book.

Interestingly, when Herbert writes of the knowledge of Scripture, what he means bears a striking resemblance to the medieval monastic practice of *lectio divina*, a meditative–contemplative reading of Scripture. In this way of understanding, there is almost a sacramental quality to Scripture. The Word of God that has the power to transform human lives is present and accessible in and through the written words, 'The Holy Scriptures (1)'. This applies first of all to the parson's own knowledge, *Country Parson*, Chapter IV. The means of knowledge is the heart which 'sucks' the words of Scripture in order to allow its 'honey' to sweeten, to heal and to enlighten. The priest is to approach Scripture always in a spirit of prayer rather than of purely intellectual enquiry.

The Bible
Readings

1 *The Country Parson*, Chapter IV

2 *The Country Parson*, Chapter VII

3 The Holy Scriptures (1)

4 The Holy Scriptures (2)

5 The 23 Psalm

6 Discipline

I

The Country Parson, Chapter IV
The Parson's Knowledge

The Country Parson is full of all knowledge. They say it is an ill mason that refuseth any stone; and there is no knowledge, but in a skilful hand serves either positively as it is, or else to illustrate some other knowledge. He condescends even to the knowledge of tillage and pasturage, and makes great use of them in teaching, because people by what they understand are best led to what they understand not. But the chief and top of his knowledge consists in the book of books, the storehouse and magazine of life and comfort, the holy Scriptures. There he sucks and lives. In the Scriptures he finds four things: Precepts for life, Doctrines for knowledge, Examples for illustration, and Promises for comfort: these he hath digested severally. But for the understanding of these; the means he useth are, first, a holy life, remembering what his Master saith, that *if any do God's will, he shall know of the doctrine, John 7*; and assuring himself that wicked men, however learned, do not know the Scriptures, because they feel them not, and because they are not understood but with the same Spirit that writ them. The second means is prayer, which if it be necessary even in temporal things, how much more in things of another world, where the well is deep, and we have nothing of ourselves to draw with? Wherefore he ever begins the reading of the Scripture with some short inward ejaculation, as, *Lord, open mine eyes, that I may see the wondrous things of thy law*, &c. The third means is a diligent collation of Scripture with Scripture. For all truth being consonant to itself, and all being penned by one and the self-same Spirit, it cannot be but that an industrious and judicious comparing of place with place must be a singular help for the right understanding of the Scriptures. To this may be added the consideration of any text with the coherence thereof, touching what goes before and what follows after, as also the scope of the Holy Ghost. When the Apostles would have called down fire from heaven, they were reproved, as ignorant of what spirit they were. For the Law required one thing, and the Gospel another: yet as diverse, not as repugnant; therefore the spirit of both is to be considered and weighed. The fourth means are commenters and fathers, who have handled the places controverted, which the parson by no means refuseth. As he doth not so study others as to neglect the grace of God in himself, and what the Holy Spirit teacheth him, so doth he assure himself that God in all ages hath had his servants, to whom he hath revealed his truth, as well as to him; and that as one country doth not bear all things that there may be a commerce, so neither hath God opened or will open all to one, that there may be a traffic in knowledge between the servants of God for the planting both of love and humility. Wherefore he hath one comment at least upon every book of Scripture, and ploughing with this and his own meditations, he enters into the secrets of God treasured in the holy Scripture.

2

The Country Parson, Chapter VII
The Parson Preaching

The Country Parson preacheth constantly: the pulpit is his joy and his throne. If he at any time intermit, it is either for want of health, or against some great festival, that he may the better celebrate it, or for the variety of the hearers, that he may be heard at his return more attentively. When he intermits, he is ever very well supplied by some able man, who treads in his steps, and will not throw down what he hath built; whom also he entreats to press some point, that he himself hath often urged with no great success, that so, in the mouth of two or three witnesses, the truth may be more established. When he preacheth he procures attention by all possible art, both by earnestness of speech (it being natural to men to think that where is much earnestness there is somewhat worth hearing), and by a diligent and busy cast of his eye on his auditors, with letting them know that he observes who marks and who not; and with particularizing of his speech – now to the younger sort, then to the elder; now to the poor, and now to the rich. This is for you, and This is for you; for particulars ever touch and awake more than generals. Herein also he serves himself of the judgments of God, as those of ancient times, so especially of the late ones; and those most which are nearest to his parish; for people are very attentive at such discourses, and think it behoves them to be so, when God is so near them, and even over their heads. Sometimes he tells them stories and sayings of others, according as his text invites him; for them also men heed and remember better then exhortations, which though earnest, yet often die with the sermon, especially with country people, which are thick and heavy, and hard to raise to a point of zeal and fervency, and need a mountain of fire to kindle them; but stories and sayings they will well remember. He often tells them that sermons are dangerous things, that none goes out of the church as he came in, but either better or worse; that none is careless before his Judge, and that the Word of God shall judge us. By these and other means the parson procures attention; but the character of his sermon is holiness: he is not witty, or learned, or eloquent, but holy; a character that Hermogenes[1] never dreamed of,

---

1 Hermogenes was a Greek writer on Rhetoric, died 180 AD.

and therefore he could give no precepts thereof. But it is gained, first, by choosing texts of devotion, not controversy, moving and ravishing texts, whereof the Scriptures are full. Secondly, by dipping and seasoning all our words and sentences in our hearts before they come into our mouths, truly affecting and cordially expressing all that we say, so that the auditors may plainly perceive that every word is heart-deep. Thirdly, by turning often, and making many apostrophes to God, as Oh Lord, bless my people and teach them this point; or Oh my Master, on whose errand I come, let me hold my peace, and do thou speak thyself, for thou art Love, and when thou teachest all are scholars. Some such irradiations scatteringly in the sermon carry great holiness in them. The prophets are admirable in this. So *Isaiah 64, Oh that thou wouldst rend the heavens, that thou wouldst come down!* &c.; and *Jeremiah* 10, after he had complained of the desolation of Israel, turns to God suddenly, *Oh Lord, I know that the way of man is not in himself,* &c. Fourthly, by frequent wishes of the people's good, and joying therein, though he himself were with St. Paul even sacrificed upon the service of their faith; for there is no greater sign of holiness than the procuring and rejoicing in another's good. And herein St. Paul excelled in all his Epistles. How did he put the Romans in all his prayers? *Rom.* 1: 9; and ceased not to give thanks for the Ephesians, *Eph.* 1: 16; and for the Corinthians 1: 4; and for the Philippians made request with joy, 1: 4; and is in contention for them whether to live or die; be with them or Christ, (verse 23); which, setting aside his care of his flock, were a madness to doubt of. What an admirable epistle is the second to the Corinthians! how full of affections! he joys and he is sorry, he grieves and he glories: never was there such care of a flock expressed, save in the great shepherd of the fold, who first shed tears over Jerusalem, and afterwards blood. Therefore this care may be learned there, and then woven into sermons, which will make them appear exceeding reverend and holy. Lastly, by an often urging of the presence and majesty of God, by these or suchlike speeches: Oh, let us all take heed what we do. God sees us, he sees whether I speak as I ought, or you hear as you ought; he sees hearts as we see faces: he is among us; for if we be here, he must be here, since we are here by him, and without him could not be here. Then turning the discourse to his majesty, And he is a great God and terrible: as great in mercy, so great in judgment. There are but two devouring elements, fire and water: he hath both in him; *his voice is as the sound of many waters (Revelation* 1[.15]); and he himself *is a consuming fire (Hebrews* 12[.29]). Such discourses show very holy.

The parson's method in handling of a text consists of two parts: first, a plain and evident declaration of the meaning of the text; and secondly, some choice observations drawn out of the whole text as it lies entire and unbroken in the Scripture itself. This he thinks natural, and sweet, and grave. Whereas the other way of crumbling a text into small parts, as, the person speaking or spoken to, the subject and object, and the like, hath neither in it sweetness, nor gravity, nor variety, since the words apart are not Scripture, but a dictionary, and may be considered alike in all the Scripture. The parson exceeds not an hour in preaching, because all ages have thought that a competency, and he that profits not in that time, will less afterwards, the same affection which made him not profit before making him then weary, and so he grows from not relishing to loathing.

3

The Holy Scriptures (1)

Oh Book! infinite sweetness! let my heart
  suck ev'ry letter, and a honey gain,
  Precious for any grief in any part;
To clear the breast, to mollify all pain.
Thou art all health, health thriving, till it make
  A full eternity: thou art a mass
  Of strange delights, where we may wish and take.
Ladies, look here; this is the thankfull glass,
That mends the looker's eyes: this is the well
  That washes what it shows. Who can endear
  Thy praise too much? thou art heav'n's Lidger here,
Working against the states of death and hell.
  Thou art joy's handsel: heav'n lies flat in thee,
  Subject to ev'ry mounter's bended knee.

4

The Holy Scriptures (2)

Oh that I knew how all thy lights combine,
    And the configurations of their glory!
    Seeing not only how each verse doth shine,
But all the constellations of the story.
This verse marks that, and both do make a motion
    Unto a third, that ten leaves off doth lie:
    Then as dispersed herbs do watch a potion,
These three make up some Christian's destiny:
Such are thy secrets, which my life makes good,
    And comments on thee: for in ev'ry thing
    Thy words do find me out, and parallels bring,
And in another make me understood.
    Stars are poor books, and oftentimes do miss:
    This book of stars lights to eternal bliss.

5

The 23 Psalm

The God of love my shepherd is,
    And he that doth me feed:
While he is mine, and I am his,
    What can I want or need?

He leads me to the tender grass,
    Where I both feed and rest;
Then to the streams that gently pass:
    In both I have the best.

Or if I stray, he doth convert
    And bring my mind in frame:
And all this not for my desert,
    But for his holy name.

Yea, in death's shady black abode
    Well may I walk, not fear:

For thou art with me; and thy rod
　To guide, thy staff to bear.

Nay, thou dost make me sit and dine,
　Ev'n in my enemies' sight:
My head with oil, my cup with wine
　Runs over day and night.

Surely thy sweet and wondrous love
　Shall measure all my days;
And as it never shall remove,
　So neither shall my praise.

6

Discipline

Throw away thy rod,
Throw away thy wrath:
　O my God,
Take the gentle path.

For my heart's desire
Unto thine is bent:
　I aspire
To a full consent.

Not a word or look
I affect to own,
　But by book,
And thy book alone.

Though I fail, I weep:
Though I halt in pace,
　Yet I creep
To the throne of grace.

Then let wrath remove;
Love will do the deed:
　For with love
Stony hearts will bleed.

Love is swift of foot;
Love's a man of war,
　　And can shoot,
And can hit from far.

Who can scape his bow?
That which wrought on thee,
　　Brought thee low,
Needs must work on me.

Throw away thy rod;
Though man frailties hath,
　　Thou art God:
Throw away thy wrath.

Liturgy

While many of the seventeenth-century Anglican writers emphasized the discipline of a spiritual life and the practices needed to sustain this, they believed above all that spirituality should be rooted not only in Scripture but also equally in the liturgy of the Church. The *Book of Common Prayer* is fundamental to an understanding of the whole period because it was in corporate worship that spiritual writers such as Herbert found their main inspiration.

The life and spirituality of the Church of England, to which Herbert gave his love and loyalty, was based firmly on corporate prayer. Unlike other Churches of the Reformation, the key foundational document of the sixteenth-century English reform was not a set of theological treatises or a catechism of belief but the *Book of Common Prayer*. This was at the heart of George Herbert's life and teaching. Archbishop Thomas Cranmer's second Prayer Book of 1552 and the 1559 Elizabethan revision familiar to Herbert was not simply a translation and radical reform of the pre-Reformation Sarum Missal. It was also a manual of teaching intended to inculcate a certain spiritual temperament or attitude of heart and mind. Herbert understood well that, in the Prayer Book, theology and faith were balanced with worship and spirituality, and the sacred was balanced with the secular. The personal side of an individual Christian's spirituality was to be shaped by living and worshipping as part of the people of God, a community that was both ecclesial and civic. The Prayer Book encouraged a rhythmic approach to life – the rhythm of the liturgical year, the monthly recitation of the Psalms and the daily two-fold Office.

There is an inherent tension in this approach to spirituality – and not an unfruitful one – between the corporate and the personal dimensions. Of course, this tension is to some extent present in all Christian traditions but within the history of the Anglican tradition it is defined in a rather specific way. The key to this lies in the actual title of the foundational document. It is a book of *common* prayer. The personal side of spirituality is allowed its importance but within the explicit context of the 'commonwealth' – the people of God. A person never prays alone. Equally the Prayer Book suggests that Christians are not called to exist solely within a gathered, purified community of right believers. This was part of the battle between supporters of the Prayer Book and what we might call 'the Puritan tendency' in Herbert's day. All the common markers of human life are touched upon in the pages of the *Book of Common Prayer* as well as special personal, collective or national needs.

The language and structure of the Prayer Book influenced all seventeenth- and eighteenth-century Anglican literature. Because of this, the spirituality is firmly liturgical. It is based on prescribed texts that came to be cherished rather than on spontaneity. Worship was understood as something determined by the Church rather than as something subjective and experiential. Worship according to the Prayer Book was also intended to be a means of unity. The same texts were to be used everywhere and by everyone whatever their personal theological positions or spiritual temperament.

It was significant for the emergence of a more coherent spiritual climate that the Church of England retained many of the traditional pre-Reformation structures such as saints' days, the cycle of the liturgical year and the rhythm of the liturgical day and week. However, there was a new stipulation that anyone who attended the service of Holy Communion should receive the sacrament. In practice, the weekly celebration desired by church leaders was rare except in some private chapels or cathedrals. The problem was that congregations were reluctant to depart from the age-old custom of infrequent reception of the sacrament. This meant that parish celebrations of Holy Communion tended to be monthly at best and often only quarterly. Yet the standard format of the weekly Sunday liturgy was drawn in part from sections of the rite of Holy Communion known as the Ante-Communion.

The insistence of the Church of England on a set liturgy was a significant factor in the eventual rejection of the ethos of the Established Church by many of the more radical Protestants. This took place during the Civil War and subsequently during the period of the Commonwealth. After the restoration of the monarchy and re-establishment of the Church of England in 1660, there were increasing moves for Non-Conformists to separate completely from the Established Church. An insistence on typical Church of England liturgical structures and formulae is very strongly evident in the writings of George Herbert.

Herbert's country parson was more than simply a weaver of words. In the tradition of the Church of England, the priest's teaching role was expressed above all else in the leadership of liturgy or other forms of public prayer. Within the spirituality implicit in the *Book of Common Prayer* public worship, whether the Offices or the Holy Communion, was to be the main school of the Lord's service. The liturgy was the foundation and privileged expression of the 'common life' of the parish as a human and religious community. For this reason, Herbert's parson was to give special attention to the dignity of public worship (*The Country Parson*, Chapter VI) and to the physical space, the church building and its furnishings, within which worship took place (*The Country Parson*, Chapter XIII). This was an essential element of the pastoral care to be exercised by the priest.

George Herbert has an understandable bias towards a spirituality based on common prayer. In *The Country Parson* there are references at various points to private prayer and also to the guidance of individual people. However, his overall belief both in his prose work and in the poems is that common prayer is, as it were, prior to any exercises of private devotion and should be the primary guide for the development of right belief, right attitudes and right action. 'Though private prayer be a brave design,/ Yet public hath more promises, more love ...' ('Perirrhanterium', lines 397–8).

The Temple contains poems that celebrate the liturgical feasts such as 'Lent' or 'Whitsunday', and others that reflect liturgical or sacramental events such as 'Antiphon', 'Mattins' or 'Even-song'. Of course there are also many explicit and implicit references to the Eucharist but they will be discussed in the section on 'Prayer'. Other liturgical references are more indirect but nonetheless clear. For example, there is no poem entitled 'Advent' but at least two poems evoke Advent themes. 'Grace' resonates with the Advent liturgy in its themes of longing and hope. The call of the poem that both grace and dew should 'Drop from above!' almost certainly refers to the words of the ancient Advent plainsong responsory, *Rorate caeli desuper et nubes pluant justum* (Drop down dew, ye heavens, from above, and let the clouds rain the Just One). It is likely, in the context, that line 21, 'O come! for thou dost know the way', also echoes the Advent hymn *Veni, Veni, Emmanuel* (O Come, O Come Emmanuel).

Access by people to Scripture, and to biblical teaching, was central to the ethos of the Church of England. However, the English Reformation made liturgy and prayer the primary context for its reading and exposition. Thus, while an intellectual or theological approach to Scripture was present, it was secondary. A theological reading of Scripture tends to address questions of belief or ethics. A liturgical or prayerful reading tends, rather, to seek resonances with human hopes and needs – not least the desire for intimacy with God.

When we turn to Herbert, can we actually separate the two great foundations of his spirituality, Scripture and the liturgy, or are they inseparable? Some commentators, reacting against what they perceive as excessively Catholic interpretations of Herbert, tend to reject liturgy as an independent context for his poems. For such writers, the Bible is the primary context for Herbert and is always a direct inspiration rather than mediated by references to the liturgy. However, several poems suggest that to distinguish sharply in this way between Scripture and the liturgy does damage to Herbert's special genius. 'The Sacrifice' is a famous example where a liturgical context for the biblical references is too explicit to be avoided. In this poem there is a particularly innovative fusion of Reformed and pre-Reformation sensibilities. Nothing in Herbert is casual or accidental. Not only does 'The Sacrifice' follow the poem entitled 'The Altar', but its cross and passion references underline a Reformation theology of the Eucharist. The Good Friday theme of 'The Sacrifice' does not refer directly to a Gospel narrative but to the ancient medieval liturgy of Holy Week. Interestingly, its use of the repetitive phrase 'Was ever grief like mine?' explicitly echoes the chanted *Improperia* or Reproaches of the pre-Reformation Sarum liturgy rather than the Prayer Book.

It seems that, at least in a few instances, the powerful significance of some of Herbert's biblical allusions would be diluted if their liturgical references were not also recognized. In the end, the Bible and the liturgy, the two great foundations of Herbert's spirituality – and indeed of the emerging Anglican spiritual tradition more generally – are too tightly interwoven to be artificially separated let alone ordered in some kind of clear priority. The peculiar genius of the British Church that Herbert celebrated depended on a creative tension between Reformed biblicism and Catholic liturgical sensibility.

Liturgy
Readings

1 *The Country Parson*, Chapter VI

2 *The Country Parson*, Chapter XIII

3 Antiphon

4 Mattins

5 Even-song

6 Grace

7 The Sacrifice

I

The Country Parson, Chapter VI
The Parson Praying

The Country Parson when he is to read divine services composeth himself to all possible reverence; lifting up his heart and hands and eyes, and using all other gestures which may express a hearty and unfeigned devotion. This he doth, first, as being truly touched and amazed with the majesty of God, before whom he then presents himself; yet not as himself alone, but as presenting with himself the whole congregation, whose sins he then bears, and brings with his own to the heavenly altar to be bathed and washed in the sacred laver of Christ's blood. Secondly, as this is the true reason of his inward fear, so he is content to express this outwardly to the utmost of his power; that being first affected himself, he may affect also his people, knowing that no sermon moves them so much to a reverence, which they forget again when they come to pray, as a devout behaviour in the very act of praying. Accordingly his voice is humble, his words treatable and slow; yet not so slow neither as to let the fervency of the supplicant hang and die between speaking, but with a grave liveliness, between fear and zeal, pausing yet pressing, he performs his duty. Besides, his example, he having often instructed his people how to carry themselves in divine service, exacts of them all possible reverence, by no means enduring either talking or sleeping, or gazing, or leaning, or half-kneeling, or any undutiful behaviour in them, but causing them when they sit, or stand, or kneel, to do all in a straight and steady posture, as attending to what is done in the Church, and every one, man and child, answering aloud both Amen and all other answers which are on the clerk's and people's part to answer, which answers also are to be done not in a huddling or slubbering fashion, gaping, or scratching the head, or spitting even in the midst of their answer, but gently and pausably, thinking what they say, so that while they answer, *As it was in the beginning*, &c., they meditate as they speak, that God hath ever had his people that have glorified him as well as now, and that he shall have so for ever. And the like in other answers. This is that which the Apostle calls a reasonable service, *Romans* 12[.1] when we speak not as parrots, without reason, or offer up such sacrifices as they did of old, which was of beasts devoid of reason; but when we use our reason, and apply our powers to the service of him that gives them. If there be any of the gentry or nobility of the parish, who sometimes make it a piece of state not to come at the beginning of service with their poor neighbours, but at mid-prayers, both to their own loss and of theirs also who gaze upon them when they come in, and neglect the present service of God, he by no means suffers it, but after divers gentle admonitions, if they persevere, he causes them to be presented: or if the poor churchwardens be affrighted with their greatness, notwithstanding his instruction that they ought not to be so, but even to let the world sink so they do their duty, he presents them himself, only protesting to them that not any ill-will draws him to it, but the debt and obligation of his calling being to obey God rather then men.

2

The Country Parson, Chapter XIII
The Parson's Church

The Country Parson hath a special care of his church, that all things there be decent, and befitting his name by which it is called. Therefore, first, he takes order that all things be in good repair; as walls plastered, windows glazed, floor paved, seats whole, firm, and uniform, especially that the pulpit, and desk, and communion table, and font, be as they ought for those great duties that are performed in them. Secondly, that the church be swept and kept clean, without dust or cobwebs, and at great festivals strewed and stuck with boughs, and perfumed with incense. Thirdly, that there be fit and proper texts of Scripture everywhere painted, and that all the painting be grave and reverend, not with light colours or foolish antics. Fourthly, that all the books appointed by authority be there, and those not torn or fouled, but whole, and clean, and well bound; and that there be a fitting and sightly communion cloth *of fine linen, with a handsome and seemly carpet of good and costly stuff or cloth, and all kept sweet and clean, in a strong and decent chest, with a chalice and cover, and a stoup or flagon, and a basin for alms and offerings; besides which he hath a poor man's box conveniently seated to receive the charity of well-minded people, and to lay up treasure for the sick and needy.* And all this he doth, not as out of necessity, or as putting a holiness in the things, but as desiring to keep the middle way between superstition and slovenliness, and as following the Apostle's two great and admirable rules in things of this nature; the first whereof is, *Let all things be done decently and in order*; the second, *Let all things be done to edification, I Cor.* 14. For these two rules comprise and include the double object of our duty, God, – and our neighbour; the first being for the honour of God; the second for the benefit of our neighbour. So that they excellently score out the way, and fully and exactly contain, even in external and indifferent things, what course is to be taken, and put them to great shame who deny the Scripture to be perfect.

3

Antiphon

    Cho. Let all the world in ev'ry corner sing
        My God and King.

    Vers. The heav'ns are not too high,
        His praise may thither fly:
        The earth is not too low,
        His praises there may grow.

    Cho. Let all the world in ev'ry corner sing,
        My God and King.

    Vers. The church with psalms must shout
        No door can keep them out:
        But above all, the heart
        Must bear the longest part.

    Cho. Let all the world in ev'ry corner sing,
        My God and King.

4

Mattins

I cannot ope mine eyes,
But thou art ready there to catch
My morning-soul and sacrifice:
Then we must needs for that day make a match.

My God, what is a heart?
Silver, or gold, or precious stone,
Or star, or rainbow, or a part
Of all these things or all of them in one?

My God, what is a heart,
That thou should'st it so eye, and woo,
Pouring upon it all thy art,
As if that thou hadst nothing else to do?

Indeed man's whole estate
Amounts (and richly) to serve thee:
He did not heav'n and earth create,
Yet studies them, not him by whom they be.

Teach me thy love to know;
That this new light, which now I see,
May both the work and workman show:
Then by a sun-beam I will climb to thee.

5

Even-song

Blest be the God of love,
Who gave me eyes, and light, and power this day,
Both to be busy, and to play.
But much more blest be God above,
Who gave me sight alone,
Which to himself he did deny:
For when he sees my ways, I die:
But I have got his son, and he hath none.

What have I brought thee home
For this thy love? have I discharg'd the debt,
  Which this day's favour did beget?
  I ran; but all I brought, was foam.
    Thy diet, care, and cost
  Do end in bubbles, balls of wind;
  Of wind to thee whom I have crost,
But balls of wild-fire to my troubled mind.

    Yet still thou goest on,
And now with darkness closest weary eyes,
  Saying to man, *It doth suffice:*
  Henceforth repose; your work is done.
    Thus in thy Ebony box
  Thou dost enclose us, till the day
  Put our amendment in our way,
And give new wheels to our disorder'd clocks.

    I muse, which shows more love,
The day or night: that is the gale, this th' harbour;
  That is the walk, and this the arbour;
  Or that the garden, this the grove.
    My God, thou art all love.
  Not one poor minute scapes thy breast,
  But brings a favour from above;
And in this love, more than in bed, I rest.

6

Grace

My stock lies dead and no increase
Doth my dull husbandry improve:
O let thy graces without cease
    Drop from above!

If still the sun should hide his face,
Thy house would but a dungeon prove,
Thy works, night's captives: O let grace
    Drop from above!

The dew doth ev'ry morning fall;
And shall the dew outstrip thy dove?
The dew, for which grass cannot call,
          Drop from above.

Death is still working like a mole,
And digs my grave at each remove:
Let grace work too, and on my soul
          Drop from above.

Sin is still hammering my heart
Unto a hardness, void of love:
Let suppling grace, to cross his art,
          Drop from above.

O come! for thou dost know the way.
Or if to me thou wilt not move,
Remove me, where I need not say,
          Drop from above.

7

The Sacrifice

Oh all ye, who pass by, whose eyes and mind
To worldly things are sharp, but to me blind;
To me, who took eyes that I might you find:
          Was ever grief like mine?

The Princes of my people make a head
Against their Maker: they do wish me dead,
Who cannot wish, except I give them bread:
          Was ever grief like mine?

Without me each one, who doth now me brave,
Had to this day been an Egyptian slave.
They use that power against me, which I gave:
          Was ever grief like mine?

Mine own Apostle, who the bag did bear,
Though he had all I had, did not forebear
To sell me also, and to put me there:
    Was ever grief like mine?

For thirty pence he did my death devise,
Who at three hundred did the ointment prize,
Not half so sweet as my sweet sacrifice:
    Was ever grief like mine?

Therefore my soul melts, and my heart's dear treasure
Drops blood (the only beads) my words to measure:
O let this cup pass, if it be thy pleasure:
    Was ever grief like mine?

These drops being temper'd with a sinner's tears,
A Balsam are for both the Hemispheres:
Curing all wounds but mine; all, but my fears,
    Was ever grief like mine?

Yet my Disciples sleep: I cannot gain
One hour of watching; but their drowsy brain
Comforts not me, and doth my doctrine stain:
    Was ever grief like mine?

Arise, arise, they come. Look how they run.
Alas! what haste they make to be undone!
How with their lanterns do they seek the sun!
    Was ever grief like mine?

With clubs and staves they seek me, as a thief,
Who am the way of truth, the true relief;
Most true to those, who are my greatest grief:
    Was ever grief like mine?

Judas, dost thou betray me with a kiss?
Canst thou find hell about my lips? and miss
Of life, just at the gates of life and bliss?
    Was ever grief like mine?

See, they lay hold on me, not with the hands
Of faith, but fury: yet at their commands
I suffer binding, who have loos'd their bands:
    Was ever grief like mine?

All my Disciples fly; fear puts a bar
Betwixt my friends and me. They leave the star
That brought the wise men of the East from far.
    Was ever grief like mine?

Then from one ruler to another bound
They lead me; urging, that it was not sound
What I taught: Comments would the text confound.
    Was ever grief like mine?

The Priest and rulers all false witness seek
'Gainst him, who seeks not life, but is the meek
And ready Paschal Lamb of this great week:
    Was ever grief like mine?

Then they accuse me of great blasphemy,
That I did thrust into the Deity,
Who never thought that any robbery:
    Was ever grief like mine?

Some said, that I the Temple to the floor
In three days raz'd, and raised as before.
Why, he that built the world can do much more:
    Was ever grief like mine?

Then they condemn me all with that same breath,
Which I do give them daily, unto death.
Thus *Adam* my first breathing rendereth:
    Was ever grief like mine?

They bind, and lead me unto *Herod:* he
Sends me to *Pilate.* This makes them agree;
But yet their friendship is my enmity:
    Was ever grief like mine?

Herod and all his bands do set me light,
Who teach all hands to war, fingers to fight,
And only am the Lord of hosts and might:
    Was ever grief like mine?

Herod in judgement sits while I do stand;
Examines me with a censorious hand:
I him obey, who all things else command:
    Was ever grief like mine?

The *Jews* accuse me with despitefulness;
And vying malice with my gentleness,
Pick quarrels with their only happiness:
    Was ever grief like mine?

I answer nothing, but with patience prove
If stony hearts will melt with gentle love.
But who does hawk at eagles with a dove?
    Was ever grief like mine?

My silence rather doth augment their cry;
My dove doth back into my bosom fly;
Because the raging waters still are high:
    Was ever grief like mine?

Hark how they cry aloud still, *Crucify:*
It is not fit he live a day, they cry,
Who cannot live less than eternally:
    Was ever grief like mine?

Pilate a stranger holdeth off; but they,
Mine own dear people, cry, *Away, away,*
With noises confused frighting the day:
    Was ever grief like mine?

Yet still they shout, and cry, and stop their ears,
Putting my life among their sins and fears,
And therefore wish *my blood on them and theirs:*
    Was ever grief like mine?

See how spite cankers things. These words aright
Used, and wished, are the whole world's light:
But honey is their gall, brightness their night:
    Was ever grief like mine?

They choose a murderer, and all agree
In him to do themselves a courtesy:
For it was their own cause who killed me:
    Was ever grief like mine?

And a seditious murderer he was:
But I the Prince of peace; peace that doth pass
All understanding, more than heav'n doth glass:
    Was ever grief like mine?

Why, Caesar is their only King, not I:
He clave the stony rock, when they were dry;
But surely not their hearts, as I well try:
    Was ever grief like mine?

Ah! how they scourge me! yet my tenderness
Doubles each lash: and yet their bitterness
Winds up my grief to a mysteriousness.
    Was ever grief like mine?

They buffet me, and box me as they list,
Who grasp the earth and heaven with my fist,
And never yet, whom I would punish, miss'd:
    Was ever grief like mine?

Behold, they spit on me in scornful wise,
Who by my spittle gave the blind man eyes,
Leaving his blindness to mine enemies:
    Was ever grief like mine?

My face they cover, though it be divine.
As *Moses'* face was veiled, so is mine,
Lest on their double-dark souls either shine:
    Was ever grief like mine?

Servants and abjects flout me; they are witty:
Now prophesy who strikes thee, is their ditty.
So they in me deny themselves all pity:
    Was ever grief like mine?

And now I am deliver'd unto death,
Which each one calls for so with utmost breath,
That he before me well nigh suffereth:
    Was ever grief like mine?

Weep not, dear friends, since I for both have wept
When all my tears were blood, the while you slept:
Your tears for your own fortunes should be kept:
    Was ever grief like mine?

The soldiers lead me to the common hall;
There they deride me, they abuse me all:
Yet for twelve heavn'ly legions I could call:
    Was ever grief like mine?

Then with a scarlet robe they me array;
Which shows my blood to be the only way.
And cordial left to repair man's decay:
    Was ever grief like mine?

Then on my head a crown of thorns I wear:
For these are all the grapes *Sion* doth bear,
Though I my vine planted and watred there:
    Was ever grief like mine?

So sits the earth's great curse in *Adam's* fall
Upon my head: so I remove it all
From th' earth unto my brows, and bear the thrall:
    Was ever grief like mine?

Then with the reed they gave to me before,
They strike my head, the rock from whence all store
Of heavn'ly blessings issue evermore:
    Was ever grief like mine?

They bow their knees to me, and cry, *Hail king:*
What ever scoffs or scornfulness can bring,
I am the floor, the sink, where they it fling:
    Was ever grief like mine?

Yet since man's sceptres are as frail as reeds,
And thorny all their crowns, bloody their weeds;
I, who am Truth, turn into truth their deeds:
    Was ever grief like mine?

The soldiers also spit upon that face,
Which Angels did desire to have the grace,
And Prophets once to see, but found no place:
    Was ever grief like mine?

Thus trimmed forth they bring me to the rout,
Who *Crucify him,* cry with one strong shout.
God holds his peace at man, and man cries out:
    Was ever grief like mine?

They lead me in once more, and putting then
Mine own clothes on, they lead me out again.
Whom devils fly, thus is he toss'd of men:
    Was ever grief like mine?

And now weary of sport, glad to engross
All spite in one, counting my life their loss,
They carry me to my most bitter cross:
    Was ever grief like mine?

My cross I bear my self, until I faint:
Then Simon bears it for me by constraint,
The decreed burden of each mortal Saint:
    Was ever grief like mine?

O all ye who pass by, behold and see;
Man stole the fruit, but I must climb the tree;
The tree of life to all, but only me:
    Was ever grief like mine?

Lo, here I hang, charg'd with a world of sin,
The greater world o' th' two; for that came in
By words, but this by sorrow I must win:
    Was ever grief like mine?

Such sorrow, as if sinful man could feel,
Or feel his part, he would not cease to kneel,
Till all were melted, though he were all steel:
    Was ever grief like mine?

But, *O my God, my God!* why leav'st thou me,
The son, in whom thou dost delight to be?
My God, my God —
    Never was grief like mine.

Shame tears my soul, my body many a wound;
Sharp nails pierce this, but sharper that confound;
Reproaches, which are free, while I am bound.
    Was ever grief like mine?

Now heal thy self, Physician; now come down.
Alas! I did so, when I left my crown
And father's smile for you, to feel his frown:
    Was ever grief like mine?

In healing not my self, there doth consist
All that salvation, which ye now resist;
Your safety in my sickness doth subsist:
    Was ever grief like mine?

Betwixt two thieves I spend my utmost breath,
As he that for some robbery suffereth.
Alas! what have I stolen from you? death:
    Was ever grief like mine?

A king my title is, prefixt on high;
Yet by my subjects am condemn'd to die
A servile death in servile company;
    Was ever grief like mine?

They gave me vinegar mingled with gall,
But more with malice: yet, when they did call,
With Manna, Angels' food, I fed them all:
　　Was ever grief like mine?

They part my garments, and by lot dispose
My coat, the type of love, which once cur'd those
Who sought for help, never malicious foes:
　　Was ever grief like mine?

Nay, after death their spite shall further go;
For they will pierce my side, I full well know;
That as sin came, so Sacraments might flow:
　　Was ever grief like mine?

But now I die; now all is finished.
My woe, man's weal: and now I bow my head.
Only let others say, when I am dead,
　　Never was grief like mine.

2

God and Jesus Christ

The reality of God is portrayed by George Herbert in terms of a challenging mixture of majesty and intimacy. Indeed, it is the intimacy of God that stands out in Herbert as one of his strongest themes. The central focus of Herbert's poetry is the nature of God and the journey of the Christian person towards God. Because of this, Herbert's richest language about God appears more strikingly in the poetry than in *The Country Parson*.

The poem 'Love (3)' (which will be considered in more detail in the section on Discipleship and Holiness) is the climax of the main section of *The Temple*. It reveals two important aspects of Herbert's understanding of God. First, God is a lover who woos the Christian soul rather than an impersonal power that seeks to impose an arbitrary and imperious will upon human beings. Second, the figure of Love in the poem is explicitly both creator ('Who made the eyes but I?') and redeemer ('Who bore the blame?'). As we shall see later, Herbert is profoundly Christ-centred. What this implies is that, while Herbert's God is infinite and ultimately beyond our understanding, God's nature is also clearly revealed in and through the life and death of Jesus Christ. Arguably, too, the Holy Spirit is at least implicitly present in the poem. Love is one of the Spirit's traditional designations and the Spirit's gift of sanctification, in which a person is made a 'guest ... worthy to be here', clearly represents the overall dynamism of the poem.

The Freedom and Majesty of God

God appears throughout Herbert's writing as free and active. Indeed the image of God as, predominantly, the active partner in the divine–human relationship runs throughout both the prose treatise and the poems. In some respects, *The Country Parson* presents a more awe-some picture of God than the poems. The parson is 'truly touched and amazed with the majesty of God' (Chapter VI). This is the approach to God that the priest is also to encourage in the congregation. The priest is continually to preach the presence and majesty of God. God is very holy, great and terrible. Yet, if God is great in judgement, God is also great in mercy (Chapter VII). Yet even here there is a tension between otherness and intimacy. His 'Prayer before Sermon' at the end of *The Country Parson* begins with a strong emphasis on the otherness of God. Yet the prayer moves forward to acknowledge that God exalts mercy above everything else. God is all-powerful. However, this power does not merely govern the created order but sustains and preserves it and turns all things to blessing and advantage. In prayer we may say to God

Of what supreme almighty power
Is thy great arm which spans the east and west,
And tacks the centre to the sphere!

Yet we must also say

Of what unmeasurable love
Art thou possest ...
                           'Prayer (2)'

At several points in the poems, Herbert is prepared to acknowledge the wrath of God, for example in poems such as 'Sighs and Groans', 'Complaining', 'Bitter-sweet'. When justified by faith in Jesus Christ, we flawed humans may look forward to the fulfilment of our vocation as creatures: union with God.

Freedom and Majesty
Readings

1 *The Country Parson*, Prayer before Sermon

2 Prayer (2)

3 Bitter-sweet

I

The Country Parson
The Author's Prayer before Sermon

O Almighty and ever-living Lord God! Majesty, and Power, and Brightness, and Glory! How shall we dare to appear before thy face, who are
contrary to thee, in all we call thee? for we are darkness, and weak-
nesses, and filthiness, and shame. Misery and sin fill our days; yet art
thou our Creator, and we thy work. Thy hands both made us, and also
made us lords of all thy creatures, giving us one world in our selves,
and another to serve us; then did'st thou place us in Paradise, and wert
proceeding still on in thy favours, until we interrupted thy counsels,
disappointed thy purposes, and sold our God, our glorious, our gracious God, for an apple. O write it! O brand it in our foreheads for
ever: for an apple once we lost our God, and still lose him for no more
– for money, for meat, for diet. But thou, Lord, art patience, and pity,
and sweetness, and love, therefore we sons of men are not consumed.
Thou hast exalted thy mercy above all things, and hast made our salvation, not our punishment, thy glory; so that then where sin abounded,
not death but grace superabounded; accordingly, when we had sinned
beyond any help in heaven or earth, then thou saidst, Lo, I come! then
did the Lord of life, unable of himself to die, contrive to do it. He took
flesh, he wept, he died; for his enemies he died, even for those that
derided him then, and still despise him. Blessed Saviour! many waters
could not quench thy love, nor no pit overwhelm it. But though the
streams of thy blood were current through darkness, grave, and hell,
yet by these thy conflicts and seemingly hazards didst thou arise triumphant and therein madest us victorious.

Neither doth thy love yet stay here! for this word of thy rich peace
and reconciliation thou hast committed, not to thunder or angels, but
to silly and sinful men; even to me, pardoning my sins, and bidding me
go feed the people of thy love.

Blessed be the God of heaven and earth! who only doth wondrous
things. Awake therefore, my lute, and my viol! awake all my powers to
glorify thee! We praise thee! we bless thee! we magnify thee for ever!
And now, O Lord! in the power of thy victories, and in the ways of thy
ordinances, and in the truth of thy love, lo, we stand here beseeching
thee to bless thy word wherever spoken this day throughout the universal Church. O make it a word of power and peace to convert those who

are not yet thine, and to confirm those that are; particularly, bless it in this thy own kingdom, which thou hast made a land of light, a store-house of thy treasures and mercies. O let not our foolish and unworthy hearts rob us of the continuance of this thy sweet love; but pardon our sins, and perfect what thou hast begun. Ride on, Lord, because of the word of truth, and meekness, and righteousness, and thy right hand shall teach thee terrible things. Especially bless this portion here assembled together, with thy unworthy servant speaking unto them. Lord Jesu! teach thou me that I may teach them. Sanctify and enable all my powers, that in their full strength they may deliver thy message reverently, readily, faithfully, and fruitfully. O make thy word a swift word, passing from the ear to the heart, from the heart to the life and conversation; that as the rain returns not empty, so neither may thy word, but accomplish that for which it is given. O Lord, hear, O Lord forgive! O Lord, harken, and do so for thy blessed Son's sake, in whose sweet and pleasing words we say, *Our Father,* &c.

2

Prayer (2)

> Of what an easy quick access,
> My blessed Lord, art thou! how suddenly
> May our requests thine ear invade!
> To show that state dislikes not easiness.
> If I but lift mine eyes, my suit is made:
> Thou canst no more not hear, than thou canst die.
>
> Of what supreme almighty power
> Is thy great arm which spans the east and west,
> And tacks the centre to the sphere!
> By it do all things live their measur'd hour:
> We cannot ask the thing, which is not there,
> Blaming the shallowness of our request.
>
> Of what unmeasurable love
> Art thou possest, who, when thou couldst not die,
> Wert fain to take our flesh and curse,
> And for our sakes in person sin reprove,
> That by destroying that which ty'd thy purse,
> Thou mightst make way for liberality!

Since then these three wait on thy throne,
Ease, *Power*, and *Love*; I value prayer so,
   That were I to leave all but one,
Wealth, fame, endowments, virtues, all should go;
I and dear prayer would together dwell,
And quickly gain, for each inch lost, an ell.

3

Bitter-sweet

Ah my dear angry Lord,
Since thou dost love, yet strike;
Cast down, yet help afford;
Sure I will do the like.

I will complain, yet praise;
I will bewail, approve:
And all my sour-sweet days
I will lament, and love.

The Loving Intimacy of God

Interestingly, God's freedom and action are most powerfully expressed not as detachment and judgement but as love. In 'Love (1)' God is 'Immortal Love' and in 'Love (2)' is addressed as 'Immortal Heat' whose 'flame' kindles in us true desires. For Herbert, God's action is always at the heart of things. Even so, human beings are not purely passive in their relationship with God. As we have already seen, the seventeenth century saw an increasing tension in Anglican circles between an emphasis on the sovereignty of God's will and human freedom and co-operation with God's action. For George Herbert, although God's action is always at the heart of things, our human response to God is equally important. Human beings are creatures of desire who (as Herbert himself appears to do in his poetry) struggle to reach out to God in response. God is the one 'who giveth me my desires and performances' (Preface to *The Country Parson*).

> For my heart's desire
> Unto thine is bent:
> 　I aspire
> To a full consent.
> 　　　　('Discipline')

Herbert understands that God woos the human soul sensitively rather than forcing or overpowering it. This enables Herbert to allow for a certain reciprocity between God and human creatures.

Although in Herbert's works, God is utterly holy ('I cannot look on thee', 'Love (3)'), his conflicts are within the context of an intimate relationship. His fundamental assurance and starting point is always God's love rather than God's judgement or wrath. God is a gracious and tolerant Father. The poem 'Sacrifice', already cited, vividly portrays the fickleness and sinfulness of humanity even in face of the cross, but God's sole response is one of generosity rather than judgement. Even the poem 'Discipline', which speaks of God's wrath, invites God to

> Throw away thy rod,
> Throw away thy wrath ...

Indeed in the final stanza of the poem Herbert seems to suggest that, because God is God, wrath is unnecessary, even inappropriate, 'Though man frailties hath'. God's love is actually more powerful and effective than anger.

> Love will do the deed:
>   For with love
> Stony hearts will bleed.

Herbert's sense of God's presence and intimacy is thoroughly incarnational. God is not removed from human life or the created world but is to be found, and responded to, in the ordinary and the everyday. Indeed, for Herbert, it is everyday events and tasks rather than the glories of nature that catch his attention most of all. God is present with the priest even as he enters the poorest cottage, 'for both God is there also, and those for whom God died' (*The Country Parson*, Chapter XIV). In the poem 'Redemption', God in Christ is to be found in the midst of 'a ragged noise and mirth/ Of thieves and murderers ...'

Nothing is outside the loving providence of God. No aspect of human life is beneath contempt. Nothing is too small for God. 'Thou art in small things great, nor small in any' ('Providence'). Herbert's spirituality of everyday life will be examined more broadly in the next section.

Apart from everyday actions and events, George Herbert experiences the presence and action of God most strongly within himself and in the celebration of the Eucharist. One of the most important images of *The Temple* is God dwelling and working within the human heart, for example in the poems entitled 'The Altar' and 'The Church-floor'. The sacramental theme is so pervasive that it would be tedious to list all the poems where the Eucharist is mentioned or implied. Herbert's eucharistic spirituality will be developed further in the chapter on prayer. Indeed, intimacy with God is often expressed sacramentally in Herbert. In 'The Agony' the association between the experience of God as Love, the cross and reception of Communion is tightly drawn. The poem makes a particularly deft connection between blood and wine that powerfully relates together God's intimacy to us, redemption and sacramental theology. The particular intimacy between God and those who preside at the Eucharist, and the burden this lays upon them, is mentioned in *The Country Parson*, Chapter XXII and in the poem 'The Priesthood'.

Perhaps the single poem that most graphically illustrates Herbert's sense of the intimacy of God is the one entitled 'Clasping of hands'. Human desire is for a union between us and God that somehow transcends 'Thine' and 'Mine'.

Loving Intimacy
Readings

I

Discipline

Throw away thy rod,
Throw away thy wrath:
 O my God,
Take the gentle path.

For my heart's desire
Unto thine is bent:
 I aspire
To a full consent.

Not a word or look
I affect to own,
 But by book,
And thy book alone.

Though I fail, I weep:
Though I halt in pace,
 Yet I creep
To the throne of grace.

Then let wrath remove;
Love will do the deed:
 For with love
Stony hearts will bleed.

Love is swift of foot;
Love's a man of war,
   And can shoot,
And can hit from far.

Who can 'scape his bow?
That which wrought on thee,
   Brought thee low,
Needs must work on me.

Throw away thy rod;
Though man frailties hath,
   Thou art God:
Throw away thy wrath!

2

The Agony

Philosophers have measur'd mountains,
Fathom'd the depths of seas, of states, and kings,
Walk'd with a staff to heav'n, and traced fountains:
   But there are two vast, spacious things,
The which to measure it doth more behove:
Yet few there are that sound them; Sin and Love.

Who would know Sin, let him repair
Unto mount Olivet; there shall he see
A man so wrung with pains, that all his hair,
   His skin, his garments bloody be.
Sin is that press and vice, which forceth pain
To hunt his cruel food though ev'ry vein.

Who knows not Love, let him assay
And taste that juice, which on the cross a pike
Did set again abroach, then let him say
   If ever he did taste the like.
Love is that liquor sweet and most divine,
Which my God feels as blood; but I, as wine.

3

Clasping of hands

Lord, thou art mine, and I am thine,
If mine I am: and thine much more,
Than I or ought, or can be mine.
Yet to be thine, doth me restore;
So that again I now am mine,
And with advantage mine the more.
Since this being mine, brings with it thine,
And thou with me doth thee restore.
  If I without thee would be mine,
  I neither should be mine nor thine.

Lord, I am thine, and thou art mine:
So mine thou art, that something more
I may presume thee mine, than thine.
For thou didst suffer to restore
Not thee, but me, and to be mine:
And with advantage mine the more,
Since thou in death wast none of thine,
Yet then as mine didst me restore.
  O be mine still! still make me thine!
  Or rather make no Thine and Mine!

The Trinity

If Herbert's God is a strange mixture of distant majesty and intimacy, how does he employ the classical Christian image of God, the Trinity? There are not many direct allusions to the Trinity in *The Temple*. There is a possible musical image in the 'three parts' of the final stanza of 'Easter'. There is a clear reference in the poem 'Trinity Sunday'. The first stanza suggests the classic three-fold titles of creator, redeemer and sanctifier.

> Lord, who hast form'd me out of mud,
> And hast redeem'd me through thy blood,
> And sanctifi'd me to do good ...

There also seem to be three triads in the final stanza that, as it were, express the desired impact or reflection of the Trinity in Herbert's life.

> Enrich my heart, mouth, hands in me,
> With faith, with hope, with charity;
> That I may run, rise, rest with thee.

Herbert's relative reticence about God as Trinity is perhaps explained in the poem 'Ungratefulness'. Here Herbert suggests that God 'hast but two rare cabinets full of treasure/ The *Trinity* and *Incarnation*'.

> The statelier cabinet is the *Trinity*,
> Whose sparkling light access denies:
>   Therefore thou dost not show
> This fully to us, till death blow
>   The dust into our eyes:
> For by that powder thou wilt make us see.

However, it is the Incarnation that can 'allure us' at this point. This is the more immediate and attractive treasure.

Certainly it is difficult to discover evidence of sharp distinctions between the traditional attributes of the persons of the Trinity. Herbert regularly changes focus from God as creator to God as redeemer. The Lord of the poem 'Longing' is 'Lord JESU', the one who died on the cross (lines 31–2). Yet the Lord is also, implicitly, the creator God ('Indeed the world's thy book', line 49). Once again, in the poem 'Redemption' it is the rich Lord of heaven who goes to earth as Son.

Trinity
Reading

1 Trinity Sunday

1

Trinity Sunday

Lord, who hast form'd me out of mud,
    And hast redeem'd me through thy blood,
    And sanctifi'd me to do good;

Purge all my sins done heretofore:
    For I confess my heavy score,
    And I will strive to sin no more.

Enrich my heart, mouth, hands in me,
    With faith, with hope, with charity;
    That I may run, rise, rest with thee.

A Christ-Centred Spirituality

In the central portion of *The Temple*, nearly all Herbert's poems concern Christ or are directly addressed to him. Christ is at the centre of the
Christian's life, carved in the human heart as in the poem 'Jesu' or bringing divine relief in 'Christmas'

Yet Herbert's Christology does not focus on the life of the human
Jesus compared to Catholic Reformation spirituality such as that of
Ignatius Loyola. This is true even when Herbert suggests that the
Christian life should reflect the double state of the life of 'our Saviour'
(*The Country Parson*, Chapter XXXIV). Herbert's emphasis is always
strongly on the cross. In 'The Bag' Christ's wounded side becomes, as
it were, the safe deposit for our messages to God. Our way to holiness is not via deluded attempts to merit God's favour (see 'Dialogue')
or through mere Christ-focused devotion, but to accept God's grace
revealed in Christ, especially in the passion, and to trust in it. Throughout all our struggles and uncertainties, our ultimate assurance is the
triumph of Christ, expressed beautifully in the poem 'Easter'.

As we have seen, Herbert tends to blend together the eternal creator
God and the suffering Christ on the cross. So, at Holy Communion
we 'receive God' (*The Country Parson*, Chapter XXII). In the poem
'Easter wings' the 'Lord, who createdst man in wealth and store' and
the Saviour are one and the same. This blending tends to outweigh any
sense of a harsh version of a penal substitution theory of the passion.
God is revealed as love rather than as a judge and this love is known
especially in Christ. The lesson of the poem 'The Sacrifice' is that we
cannot finally defeat God's love. Even our refusals of love merely serve
to reveal further depths of love in God's patient endurance. Herbert's
frequent use of the title 'Lord' for God is not, therefore, a matter of
power. Indeed God seems closest when met precisely as the Lord who
is courteous or who, for example in the poem 'Redemption', does a
favour or grants a suit. There is even a modest hint of a feminine image
for God in the poem 'Longing' where, as in Julian of Norwich, human
motherhood is a reflection of God.

> From thee all pity flows.
> Mothers are kind, because thou art,
> And dost dispose
> To them a part:

Their infants, them, and they suck thee
    More free.

Christ-Centred Reading

1 Jesu

2 Christmas

3 Dialogue

1

Jesu

Jesu is in my heart, his sacred name
Is deeply carved there: but th' other week
A great affliction broke the little frame,
Ev'n all to pieces, which I went to seek:
And first I found the corner, where was *J*,
After, where *E S*, and next where *U* was graved.
When I had got these parcels, instantly
I sat me down to spell them, and perceived
That to my broken heart he was *I ease you*,
    And to my whole is *JESU*.

2

Christmas

All after pleasures as I rid one day,
    My horse and I, both tir'd, body and mind,
    With full cry of affections, quite astray,
I took up in the next inn I could find.
There when I came, whom found I but my dear,
    My dearest Lord, expecting till the grief
    Of pleasures brought me to him, ready there
To be all passengers' most sweet relief?

O Thou, whose glorious, yet contracted light,
   Wrapt in night's mantle, stole into a manger;
   Since my dark soul and brutish is thy right,
To Man of all beasts be not thou a stranger:
   Furnish and deck my soul, that thou mayst have
   A better lodging, than a rack, or grave.

The shepherds sing; and shall I silent be?
   My God, no hymn for thee?
My soul's a shepherd too; a flock it feeds
   Of thoughts, and words, and deeds,
The pasture is thy word: the streams, thy grace
   Enriching all the place.
Shepherd and flock shall sing, and all my powers
   Out-sing the day-light hours.
Then we will chide the sun for letting night
   Take up his place and right:
We sing one common Lord; wherefore he should
   Himself the candle hold.
I will go searching, till I find a sun
   Shall stay, till we have done;
A willing shiner, that shall shine as gladly,
   As frost-nipt suns look sadly.
Then we will sing, and shine all our own day,
   And one another pay:
His beams shall cheer my breast, and both so twine,
Till ev'n his beams sing, and my music shine.

3

Dialogue

Sweetest Saviour, if my soul
   Were but worth the having,
Quickly should I then control
   Any thought of waiving.
But when all my care and pains
Cannot give the name of gains
To thy wretch so full of stains,
What delight or hope remains?

I

The Search

Whither, O, whither art thou fled,
　My Lord, my Love?
My searches are my daily bread;
　Yet never prove.

My knees pierce th' earth, mine eyes the sky;
　And yet the sphere
And centre both to me deny
　That thou art there.

Yet can I mark how herbs below
　Grow green and gay,
As if to meet thee they did know,
　While I decay.

Yet can I mark how stars above
　Simper and shine,
As having keys unto thy love,
　While poor I pine.

I sent a sigh to seek thee out,
　Deep drawn in pain,
Wing'd like an arrow: but my scout
　Returns in vain.

I tun'd another (having store)
　Into a groan,
Because the search was dumb before:
　But all was one.

Lord, dost thou some new fabric mould
　Which favour wins,
And keeps thee present, leaving th' old
　Unto their sins?

Where is my God? what hidden place
   Conceals thee still?
What covert dare eclipse thy face?
   Is it thy will?

O let not that of any thing;
   Let rather brass,
Or steel, or mountains be thy ring,
   And I will pass.

Thy will such an entrenching is,
   As passeth thought:
To it all strength, all subtleties
   Are things of nought.

Thy will such a strange distance is,
   As that to it
East and West touch, the poles do kiss,
   And parallels meet.

Since then my grief must be as large,
   As is thy space,
Thy distance from me; see my charge,
   Lord, see my case.

O take these bars, these lengths away;
   Turn, and restore me:
Be not Almighty, let me say,
   Against, but for me.

When thou dost turn, and wilt be near;
   What edge so keen,
What point so piercing can appear
   To come between?

For as thy absence doth excel
   All distance known:
So doth thy nearness bear the bell,
   Making two one.

2

Denial

When my devotions could not pierce
    Thy silent ears;
Then was my heart broken, as was my verse:
  My breast was full of fears
    And disorder:

My bent thoughts, like a brittle bow,
    Did fly asunder:
Each took his way; some would to pleasures go,
  Some to the wars and thunder
    Of alarms.

As good go any where, they say,
    As to benumb
Both knees and heart, in crying night and day,
  Come, come, my God, O come,
    But no hearing.

O that thou shouldst give dust a tongue
    To cry to thee,
And then not hear it crying! all day long
  My heart was in my knee,
    But no hearing.

Therefore my soul lay out of sight,
    Untun'd, unstrung:
My feeble spirit, unable to look right,
  Like a nipt blossom, hung
    Discontented.

O cheer and tune my heartless breast,
    Defer no time;
That so thy favours granting my request,
  They and my mind may chime,
    And mend my rhyme.

3

Longing

With sick and famisht eyes,
With doubling knees and weary bones,
    To thee my cries,
    To thee my groans,
To thee my sighs, my tears ascend:
        No end?

My throat, my soul is hoarse;
My heart is wither'd like a ground
    Which thou dost curse.
    My thoughts turn round,
And make me giddy; Lord, I fall,
        Yet call.

From thee all pity flows.
Mothers are kind, because thou art,
    And dost dispose
    To them a part:
Their infants, them; and they suck thee
        More free.

Bowels of pity, hear!
Lord of my soul, love of my mind,
    Bow down thine ear!
    Let not the wind
Scatter my words, and in the same
        Thy name!

Look on my sorrows' round!
Mark well my furnace! O what flames,
    What heats abound!
    What griefs, what shames!
Consider, Lord; Lord, bow thine ear,
        And hear!

Lord Jesu, thou didst bow
Thy dying head upon the tree:
    O be not now
    More dead to me!
Lord hear! *Shall he that made the ear,*
     Not hear?

    Behold, thy dust doth stir,
It moves, it creeps, it aims at thee:
    Wilt thou defer
    To succour me,
Thy pile of dust, wherein each crumb
    Says, Come?

    To thee help appertains.
Hast thou left all things to their course,
    And laid the reins
    Upon the horse?
Is all lockt? hath a sinner's plea
    No key?

    Indeed the world's thy book,
Where all things have their leaf assign'd:
    Yet a meek look
    Hath interlin'd.
Thy board is full, yet humble guests
    Find nests.

    Thou tarriest, while I die,
And fall to nothing: thou dost reign,
    And rule on high,
    While I remain
In bitter grief: yet am I stil'd
    Thy child.

    Lord, didst thou leave thy throne,
Not to relieve? how can it be,
    That thou art grown
    Thus hard to me?
Were sin alive, good cause there were
    To bear.

But now both sin is dead,
And all thy promises live and bide.
    That wants his head;
    These speak and chide,
And in thy bosom pour my tears,
      As theirs.

Lord JESU, hear my heart,
Which hath been broken now so long,
    That ev'ry part
    Hath got a tongue!
Thy beggars grow; rid them away
      Today.

My love, my sweetness, hear!
By these thy feet, at which my heart
    Lies all the year,
    Pluck out thy dart,
And heal my troubled breast which cries,
      Which dies.

3

Incarnational Spirituality

We have already seen that George Herbert, like so many early representatives of the Anglican spiritual tradition, had a strong sense of God's presence in the world and of God's involvement with the human condition. For this reason, seventeenth-century Anglican spirituality has often been described as particularly 'incarnational'. Its central emphasis is that God is committed to the world as creator and this commitment is further underlined in God's action of redeeming the world in Christ. The God of Christianity is thoroughly engaged with time and space rather than detached from them. These perspectives affirm something vital about God. But the notion of an incarnate God also says something very important about the value of the material world and of everyday human life. The whole of human existence, our minds and bodies as well as our spiritual dimension, are gifts of God. The world is the theatre of God's activity and a place of soul making rather than simply an unhappy vale of tears. Nothing is unimportant to God and, for us humans, everything has the capacity to unlock eternity.

As we shall see, Herbert does give some attention to the natural world as a second book of revelation alongside the Scriptures. However, compared to other well-known seventeenth-century Anglican writers such as Thomas Traherne or Henry Vaughan, Herbert's attention is focused less on the sacred quality of nature or landscape and rather more on finding God in everyday *events* and in human *action*. As we shall see in the next chapter, even Herbert's sense of place is closely associated with the life and activities of specific communities of people.

A Spirituality of Time

A concern to seek and find God in the everyday necessarily involves viewing time as important. Because Herbert's spirituality is so liturgical it is hardly surprising that for him time is imbued with spiritual significance. Although his poem 'Time' suggests an ambivalent attitude on his part, it certainly suggests that, because of Christ's coming, time is no longer the destroyer of human aspirations. Time has become the gardener who prunes us so that we might grow properly and moves us towards union with God.

It has sometimes been suggested that the doctrine of Christ's resurrection destroys time. However, a Christian view of time cannot view it as ultimately valueless. Christ's resurrection overcomes time only as *a symbol of the destruction of human hopes and meaning*. Time, itself, is not so much destroyed as transfigured and given a wholly new significance. Herbert hints at this when he suggests that time is now the channel that draws us inexorably towards a destiny that is full of promise.

The liturgical sensibilities of Anglicanism that Herbert so deeply shared have always given significant attention to the importance of time in the shaping of spirituality. Of course this is also thoroughly biblical because the origins of liturgy lie in the Jewish roots of Christianity and, as Abraham Heschel suggested so beautifully in his book *The Sabbath*, Judaism is a religion of time. Time is the architecture of holiness because it is there that human beings can discover the reality of eternity with which time is imbued. At the most basic level, the spiritual significance of time is underlined and shaped in the celebration of liturgical seasons and festivals, in the daily rhythm of common prayer, in the cycle of Scripture readings and in the monthly cycle for the recitation of the Psalms. In a general sense, the liturgical attention to time is intended to connect our relationship with time to the overall process of our daily lives.

However, there is a deeper level to the spirituality of time that Herbert was able to enter through the liturgy as much as through the Bible. Liturgy, and especially the Eucharist, brings our particular moment of time into living contact with all time; past, present and future. Time and eternity intersect in this moment of communion. It becomes 'heaven in ordinary'. Thus, in his poem 'Sunday', Herbert suggests that this particular weekly time, associated with public liturgy, is a kind of doorway from ordinary time to eternity. This somehow anticipates the time of our own death, that ultimate doorway into eternal life. Thus, Herbert suggests, the year of our lives that is most fruitful is the one which brings the ultimate harvesting 'when we leave our corn and hay' and also encounter 'The last and lov'd, though dreadful day' ('Home').

Time
Readings

1 Time

2 Sunday

I

Time

Meeting with Time, slack thing, said I,
Thy scythe is dull; whet it for shame.
No marvel Sir, he did reply,
If it at length deserve some blame:
    But where one man would have me grind it,
    Twenty for one too sharp do find it.

Perhaps some such of old did pass,
Who above all things lov'd this life;
To whom thy scythe a hatchet was,
Which now is but a pruning-knife.
    Christ's coming hath made man thy debtor,
    Since by thy cutting he grows better.

And in his blessing thou art blest:
For where thou only wert before
An executioner at best;
Thou art a gard'ner now, and more,
    An usher to convey our souls
    Beyond the utmost stars and poles.

And this is that makes life so long,
While it detains us from our God.

Ev'n pleasures here increase the wrong,
And length of days lengthen the rod.
　　Who wants the place, where God doth dwell,
　　Partakes already half of hell.

Of what strange length must that needs be,
Which ev'n eternity excludes!
Thus far Time heard me patiently:
Then chafing said, This man deludes:
　　What do I here before his door?
　　He doth not crave less time, but more.

2

Sunday

　　O day most calm, most bright,
The fruit of this, the next world's bud,
Th' endorsement of supreme delight,
Writ by a friend, and with his blood;
The couch of time; care's balm and bay:
The week were dark, but for thy light:
　　Thy torch doth show the way.

　　The other days and thou
Make up one man; whose face thou art,
Knocking at heaven with thy brow:
The worky-days are the back-part;
The burden of the week lies there,
Making the whole to stoop and bow,
　　Till thy release appear.

　　Man had straight forward gone
To endless death: but thou dost pull
And turn us round to look on one,
Whom, if we were not very dull,
We could not choose to look on still;
Since there is no place so alone,
　　The which he doth not fill.

Sundays the pillars are,
On which heav'n's palace arched lies:
The other days fill up the spare
And hollow room with vanities.
They are the fruitful beds and borders
In God's rich garden: that is bare,
    Which parts their ranks and orders.

    The Sundays of man's life,
Threaded together on time's string,
Make bracelets to adorn the wife
Of the eternal glorious King.
On Sunday heaven's gate stands ope;
Blessings are plentiful and rife,
    More plentiful than hope.

    This day my Saviour rose,
And did enclose this light for his:
That, as each beast his manger knows,
Man might not of his fodder miss.
Christ hath took in this piece of ground,
And made a garden there for those
    Who want herbs for their wound.

    The rest of our Creation
Our great Redeemer did remove
With the same shake, which at his passion
Did th' earth and all things with it move.
As Samson bore the doors away,
Christ's hands, though nail'd, wrought our salvation,
    And did unhinge that day.

    The brightness of that day
We sullied by our foul offence:
Wherefore that robe we cast away,
Having a new at his expence,
Whose drops of blood paid the full price,
That was requir'd to make us gay,
    And fit for Paradise.

Thou art a day of mirth:
And where the week-days trail on ground,
Thy flight is higher, as thy birth.
O let me take thee at the bound,
Leaping with thee from sev'n to sev'n,
Till that we both, being toss'd from earth,
　Fly hand in hand to heav'n!

The Created World

Without doubt, Herbert appreciated the natural world as a context for experiencing the presence and activity of God. He does not simply describe the beauty of nature in different poems but employs natural images in other ways. In an interesting link between time and the natural world, Sunday, according to his poem already cited, is 'the next world's bud'. The other days of the week 'are the fruitful beds and borders/ In God's rich garden'. And God's rich garden is the natural world. The month of May 'straw'd with flow'rs and happiness' becomes a striking image of Herbert's fresh and youthful faith before he entered into a deeper spiritual struggle ('Affliction (1)'). Most powerfully, when God's presence comes alive again for us after periods of spiritual darkness, snow melting in May and the flowering of springtime provide the evocative images ('The Flower').

Herbert has a particular fondness for the imagery of bees and herbs. Bees represent productive lives, not least when Herbert expresses his deep desire to serve God usefully ('Employment (1)') or when he laments his spiritual weakness. Bees also become an image of the natural wisdom that all creatures have that enables God's providence to express itself effectively in the world's workings ('Providence'). Heaven may be compared to a hive to which our lives are drawn like laden bees ('The Star').

For all that Herbert relishes natural imagery and offers a positive view of the created order, his vision is not merely romantic or a form of nature mysticism. Creation is the second book of revelation precisely because it draws us to the deeper truth of God's reality, loving presence and powerful action ('Longing').

The poem 'Misery' not only expresses Herbert's deep sense of nature as a revelation of God but also the danger of overlooking the presence of the Creator within the created order and of confining our wonder to what is partial rather extending it to what is All. Herbert's mystical sense is always focused beyond the immediate, beyond the appearance of things, to the ultimate source of beauty and goodness. There are undoubtedly echoes here of the Wisdom literature of the Hebrew Scriptures of which Herbert was particularly fond, if not an explicit allusion to the Wisdom of Solomon, 13.1–9.

Created World
Readings

1

The Flower

How fresh, O Lord, how sweet and clean
Are thy returns! ev'n as the flowers in spring;
   To which, besides their own demean,
The late-past frosts tributes of pleasures bring.
     Grief melts away
     Like snow in May,
   As if there were no such cold thing.

Who would have thought my shrivel'd heart
Could have recover'd greenness? It was gone
   Quite under ground; as flowers depart
To see their mother-root, when they have blown;
     Where they together
     All the hard weather,
   Dead to the world, keep house unknown.

These are thy wonders, Lord of power,
Killing and quickning, bringing down to hell
   And up to heaven in an hour;
Making a chiming of a passing-bell.
     We say amiss,
     This or that is:
   Thy word is all, if we could spell.

O that I once past changing were,
Fast in thy Paradise, where no flower can wither!

Many a spring I shoot up fair,
Offring at heav'n, growing and groaning thither:
    Nor doth my flower
    Want a spring-shower,
My sins and I joining together:

But while I grow in a straight line,
Still upwards bent, as if heav'n were mine own,
   Thy anger comes, and I decline:
What frost to that? what pole is not the zone,
    Where all things burn,
    When thou dost turn,
And the least frown of thine is shown?

And now in age I bud again,
After so many deaths I live and write;
   I once more smell the dew and rain,
And relish versing: O my only light,
    It cannot be
    That I am he
On whom thy tempests fell all night.

These are thy wonders, Lord of love,
To make us see we are but flowers that glide:
   Which when we once can find and prove,
Thou hast a garden for us, where to bide.
    Who would be more,
    Swelling through store,
Forfeit their Paradise by their pride.

2

Employment (1)

If as a flower doth spread and die,
   Thou wouldst extend me to some good,
Before I were by frost's extremity
    Nipt in the bud;

The sweetness and the praise were thine;
But the extension and the room,
Which in thy garland I should fill, were mine
At thy great doom.

For as thou dost impart thy grace,
The greater shall our glory be.
The measure of our joys is in this place,
The stuff with thee.

Let me not languish then, and spend
A life as barren to thy praise,
As is the dust, to which that life doth tend,
But with delays.

All things are busy; only I
Neither bring honey with the bees,
Nor flowers to make that, nor the husbandry
To water these.

I am no link of thy great chain,
But all my company is a weed.
Lord place me in thy consort; give one strain
To my poor reed.

3

Misery

Lord, let the Angels praise thy name.
Man is a foolish thing, a foolish thing,
Folly and Sin play all his game.
His house still burns, and yet he still doth sing,
Man is but grass,
He knows it, fill the glass.

How canst thou brook his foolishness?
Why he'll not lose a cup of drink for thee:
Bid him but temper his excess;
Not he: he knows, where he can better be,

As he will swear,
Than to serve thee in fear.

What strange pollutions doth he wed,
And make his own? as if none knew, but he.
No man shall beat into his head
That thou within his curtains drawn canst see:
They are of cloth,
Where never yet came moth.

The best of men, turn but thy hand
For one poor minute, stumble at a pin:
They would not have their actions scann'd,
Nor any sorrow tell them that they sin,
Though it be small,
And measure not their fall.

They quarrel thee, and would give over
The bargain made to serve thee: but thy love
Holds them unto it, and doth cover
Their follies with the wing of thy mild Dove,
Not suff'ring those
Who would, to be thy foes.

My God, Man cannot praise thy name:
Thou art all brightness, perfect purity;
The sun holds down his head for shame,
Dead with eclipses, when we speak of thee:
How shall infection
Presume on thy perfection?

As dirty hands foul all they touch,
And those things most, which are most pure and fine:
So our clay hearts, ev'n when we crouch
To sing thy praises, make them less divine.
Yet either this,
Or none thy portion is.

Man cannot serve thee; let him go,
And serve the swine: there, there is his delight:

He doth not like this virtue, no;
Give him his dirt to wallow in all night:
　　These Preachers make
　　　His head to shoot and ache.

Oh foolish man! where are thine eyes?
How hast thou lost them in a crowd of cares?
　　Thou pull'st the rug, and wilt not rise,
No not to purchase the whole pack of stars:
　　　There let them shine,
　　　Thou must go sleep, or dine.

The bird that sees a dainty bower
Made in the tree, where she was wont to sit,
　　Wonders and sings, but not his power
Who made the arbour: this exceeds her wit.
　　　But Man doth know
　　　The spring, whence all things flow:

And yet, as though he knew it not,
His knowledge winks, and lets his humours reign;
　　They make his life a constant blot,
And all the blood of God to run in vain.
　　　Ah wretch! what verse
　　　Can thy strange ways rehearse?

Indeed at first Man was a treasure,
A box of jewels, shop of rarities,
　　A ring, whose posy was, *My pleasure:*
He was a garden in a Paradise:
　　　Glory and grace
　　　Did crown his heart and face.

But sin hath fool'd him. Now he is
A lump of flesh, without a foot or wing
　　To raise him to the glimpse of bliss:
A sick toss'd vessel, dashing on each thing;
　　　Nay, his own shelf:
　　　My God, I mean my self.

The Everyday

Herbert belongs to a broad tradition of spirituality that places most emphasis on seeking and finding God in the ordinary and everyday. It is tempting to seek direct connections between George Herbert and those Roman Catholic spiritualities that were known in England in his day. For example, those associated with Ignatius Loyola or Francis de Sales had a similar emphasis on finding God in everyday life. It is likely that Herbert, like his friend Nicholas Ferrar, was aware of de Sales. However, Herbert's preoccupation with the everyday is just as likely to be rooted partly in his strong liturgical sense and partly in Reformation sensitivities. The latter tended to emphasize first of all engagement with God in the ordinary rather than in mystical illuminations, then a certain equality of experience among Christians that tended to favour everyday contexts, and finally a strong sense that our relationship with God would be expressed in moral action. Thus the long poem 'Perirrhanterium' that forms the bulk of the first section of *The Temple*, entitled 'The Church Porch', is often seen as relatively uninspiring and moral in tone. Yet it also establishes a firm foundation for the more personal struggles in the later poems by focusing our attention on the events of daily life and on concern for other people.

However, undoubtedly the best-known example in Herbert of a spirituality of the everyday is the words of what became known as the hymn 'Teach me my God and King', called 'The Elixir' in Herbert's collection. On the one hand, the magic formula, the alchemist's stone, is simply to do everything, however small, as an act of praise of God. There are parallels here to the great Carmelite mystics Teresa of Avila and Brother Lawrence and their spirituality of finding God among the pots. Nothing is too ordinary and nothing too small to be the focus for our contemplative vision. However, the sense of the final stanza is richer still. God does not 'touch' the ordinary in a simple sense. 'To touch' in reference to fine metals such as gold refers to the touchstone used to test the purity of the metal. Equally, once 'touched' (that is, tested), the metals were marked with their standard of purity. So, our 'ordinary' existence lived out for God is tested and accepted by God and declared to be pure gold.

The Everyday Reading

1 The Elixir

I

The Elixir

Teach me, my God and King,
　　In all things thee to see,
And what I do in any thing,
　　To do it as for thee:

Not rudely, as a beast,
　　To run into an action;
But still to make thee prepossest,
　　And give it his perfection.

A man that looks on glass,
　　On it may stay his eye;
Or if he pleaseth, through it pass,
　　And then the heav'n espy.

All may of thee partake:
　　Nothing can be so mean,
Which with his tincture (for thy sake)
　　Will not grow bright and clean.

A servant with this clause
　　Makes drudgery divine:
Who sweeps a room, as for thy laws,
　　Makes that and th' action fine.

This is the famous stone
　　That turneth all to gold:
For that which God doth touch and own
　　Cannot for less be told.

Beauty, Music and Poetry

George Herbert was someone with deep aesthetic sensibilities. We have already seen how he appreciated the beauties of liturgy and of church buildings and their power to make an impact on the human spirit. Apart from the imaginative qualities of his own poetry, we know that Herbert had a deep love of music and was an able musician in his own right, as noted by Isaak Walton in his *The Life of Mr George Herbert*. He had a particular appreciation of church music which he suggested was 'the way to heaven's door' ('Church-music').

Clearly Herbert felt the need to justify his love and practice of music against the more stringent Puritan party within the Church. His prose text *The Country Parson* offers few examples of this sensitivity. It is essentially a didactic and moralistic text and its austere tone hardly expresses Herbert's own creative abilities. We have to turn to Herbert's poems for any real indication of this side of his temperament and spirituality. In *The Temple* musical images abound and it is possible to make only a small selection to give a flavour of Herbert's vision.

Musical imagery (and possibly a reference to his actual music-making) is used to express Herbert's intense desire to respond to Christ's grief and passion ('The Thanksgiving'). Herbert found that musical images had a particular power to express praise of God. In the poem 'Praise (2)', which became a popular hymn, Herbert promises 'Wherefore with my utmost art/ I will sing thee'. In the poem 'Easter', in a more extended musical reference, Herbert greets the risen Easter Lord with the image of lute playing. Christ's arms stretched on the cross are compared to the taut strings of the lute that are tuned to just the right pitch to make the appropriate notes. Herbert calls on God's Spirit to 'bear a part' and thus enrich the imperfect harmony of human attempts to praise God.

The image of tuning an instrument is also used to express the ways that God seeks to enable the growth of human sinners ('The Temper (1)'). Equally, Herbert uses the image of tuning for moments when he suffered from spiritual dryness. His soul was 'untun'd, unstrung' and he begs God to 'mend my rhyme' and to 'cheer and tune my heartless breast' ('Denial').

Herbert thought of poetry as itself a form of prayer. Interestingly, lyric poetry underwent a particularly important moment of development at the time that Herbert was writing. Lyric verse had particular associations with love poetry and also with movement or change. Both of these associations were taken and used by Herbert as a means of portraying the seasons of the soul and the intensity of his love relationship with God. At times, poetry seems scarcely adequate to praise God. 'To write a verse or two is all the praise/ That I can raise' ('Praise (1)'). For all its limitations, however, Herbert is able to declare that poetry is a means of communion with God. 'But it is that which while I use/ I am with thee' ('The Quiddity').

Behind Herbert's aesthetic appreciation lies a sense of the beauty of God. Herbert's appreciation of created beauty is expressed less in terms of aesthetics pure and simple and more in terms of the ways creation reflects the beauty of God. It is humankind's particular gift to be able to discern the presence of God in all things. To praise the beauty and value of human activities such as making music or writing poetry was also to praise God. On the other hand, the beauty of human phrases or compositions is merely a pale reflection of God's beauty. 'True beauty dwells on high: ours is a flame/ But borrow'd thence to light us thither' ('The Forerunners'). Thus, for all that Herbert loved music so deeply, in the end he would affirm that 'Christ is my only head,/ My alone only heart and breast,/ My only music' ('Aaron').

Beauty
Readings

1 Church-music

2 The Thanksgiving

3 Easter

I

Church-music

Sweetest of sweets, I thank you: when displeasure
   Did through my body wound my mind,
You took me thence, and in your house of pleasure
   A dainty lodging me assign'd.

Now I in you without a body move,
 Rising and falling with your wings:
We both together sweetly live and love,
 Yet say sometimes, *God help poor Kings.*

Comfort, I'll die; for if you post from me,
 Sure I shall do so, and much more:
But if I travel in your company,
 You know the way to heaven's door.

2

The Thanksgiving

Oh King of grief! (a title strange, yet true,
 To thee of all kings only due)
Oh King of wounds! how shall I grieve for thee,
 Who in all grief preventest me?
Shall I weep blood ? why thou hast wept such store,
 That all thy body was one door.
Shall I be scourged, flouted, boxed, sold?
 'Tis but to tell the tale is told.
My God, my God, why dost thou part from me?
 Was such a grief as cannot be.
Shall I then sing, skipping, thy doleful story,
 And side with thy triumphant glory?
Shall thy strokes be my stroking? thorns, my flower?
 Thy rod, my posy? cross, my bower?
But how then shall I imitate thee, and
 Copy thy fair, though bloody hand?
Surely I will revenge me on thy love,
 And try who shall victorious prove.
If thou dost give me wealth, I will restore
 All back unto thee by the poor.
If thou dost give me honour, men shall see,
 The honour doth belong to thee.
I will not marry; or, if she be mine,
 She and her children shall be thine.
My bosom friend, if he blaspheme thy name,
 I will tear thence his love and fame.

One half of me being gone, the rest I give
    Unto some Chapel, die or live.
As for thy passion – but of that anon,
    When with the other I have done.
For thy predestination I'll contrive,
    That three years hence, if I survive,
I'll build a spittle, or mend common ways,
    But mend my own without delays.
Then I will use the works of thy creation,
    As if I us'd them but for fashion.
The world and I will quarrel; and the year
    Shall not perceive, that I am here.
My music shall find thee, and ev'ry string
    Shall have his attribute to sing;
That all together may accord in thee,
    And prove one God, one harmony.
If thou shalt give me wit, it shall appear;
    If thou hast giv'n it me, 'tis here.
Nay, I will read thy book, and never move
    Till I have found therein thy love;
Thy art of love, which I'll turn back on thee,
    O my dear Saviour, Victory!
Then for thy passion – I will do for that –
    Alas, my God, I know not what.

3

Easter

Rise heart; thy Lord is risen. Sing his praise
    Without delays,
Who takes thee by the hand, that thou likewise
    With him mayst rise:
That, as his death calcined thee to dust,
His life may make thee gold, and much more just.

Awake, my lute, and struggle for thy part
    With all thy art.
The cross taught all wood to resound his name,
    Who bore the same.

His stretched sinews taught all strings, what key
Is best to celebrate this most high day.

Consort both heart and lute, and twist a song
    Pleasant and long:
Or since all music is but three parts vied
    And multiplied,
O let thy blessed Spirit bear a part,
And make up our defects with his sweet art.

I got me flowers to straw thy way;
I got me boughs off many a tree:
But thou wast up by break of day,
And brought'st thy sweets along with thee.

The Sun arising in the East,
Though he give light, and th' East perfume;
If they should offer to contest
With thy arising, they presume.

Can there be any day but this,
Though many suns to shine endeavour?
We count three hundred, but we miss:
There is but one, and that one ever.

4

Sense of Place

A sense of place or locality is central to George Herbert's spiritual vision. It is an important key to his description of the localized ministry of the country parson. An emphasis on the church building as sacred place also acts as one of the frameworks for the major collection of poems, *The Temple*.

There is an intimate connection between our sense of place and a re-alization of God 'placed' in the heart of human life. The Anglican spir-itual tradition has expressed a particularly strong sense of place. Some commentators have pointed to close connections between the under-standing of liturgy and of the worshipping community in the *Book of Common Prayer* and the unusual degree of influence of Benedictine monasticism on the English Church due to the monastic administration of more than half the cathedrals prior to the Reformation. So perhaps 'place' in Herbert has something to do with a residual, if unconscious, echo of the monastic virtue of stability. However, there are probably more immediate reasons. The obvious one is that the Church of Eng-land was heir to the pre-Reformation pattern of geographical parishes. It continued to stand for a community model of Church rather than for the gathered or associational model that inevitably came to be the norm for dissenters, whether Puritans or persecuted Roman Catholics. Again, the Church of England model of priesthood was not something that existed in its own right in theological isolation but was grounded in relationship to a specific local community where the Word of God was preached and the sacraments celebrated. In a more general way, Anglican identity from the beginning was not based on tightly defined doctrine or innovative structures but rather on a sense of shared history and present connections. In other words, the Church of England had a great deal to do with community life, which meant people and places – indeed, people *in* places.

A sense of place is as closely linked to human relations as it is to physical landscapes. A vital part of Herbert's vision of 'place' concerns human and religious *community*. 'Community' is a key element of Herbert's spirituality. It is first and foremost a rooted community, based on the particular places where people may find home – whether that is a family household or a village. Within Herbert's vision of community there is a careful balance of prayer, study and recreation. At the heart of it lies a strong sense of shared history that links together a sense of place and a sense of time. This is probably one reason why Herbert appears to prize so highly ancient customs as well as regularity and rhythm. Individual people find their identity by slipping into this stream of history. Religiously, this 'community history' is shaped by liturgy. This offers a rhythm for days and seasons. It allows space for the personal. Yet liturgy also insists that people's stories, at any given moment, are essentially reinforced not only by being intertwined with the stories of other people past, present and future but also by means of an encounter between all these stories and God's story in Christ. For Herbert, in the Church's liturgy, *this* time and *this* place connect with all time and all places. In fact, the same may be said of the 'liturgy' of everyday events and everyday relationships in which Herbert equally believed that eternity and God could be found. Inevitably, an experience of community shaped by worship not only draws people out of themselves but, collectively, leads the community as a whole beyond parochialism. At root, Herbert's sense of community does not exist simply to reflect the preoccupations of its own place or to service its own concerns. True Christian community is a place of hospitality and also a place out of which comes a strong sense of service.

The Household

A vision of home, family and household is an important theme in Herbert's *The Country Parson*. According to Herbert, the priest's household, like the monastery of *The Rule of St Benedict* (Prologue 45), is a 'school of the Lord's service'. It is a place of spiritual nurture, education, ministry and hospitality as well as a context for establishing a proper rhythm for living. Parents, children, servants and guests share in a balanced and rhythmic life of prayer, study, sober recreation and the service of neighbour. Although Herbert lived in a post-monastic Church, one cannot help wondering whether the form of community life practised by his great friend Nicholas Ferrar and his family at Little Gidding had some influence. Influences are difficult to ascertain although Ferrar appears to have encountered Anabaptist communities as well as Roman Catholic religious during his travels on the continent. It is also just possible that both men were aware of the teaching on the 'mixed life' (contemplation and action) written for reform-minded clergy and devout lay people by the fourteenth-century spiritual teacher Walter Hilton. There is some evidence that Hilton's writings continued to circulate in England after the Reformation and may have been accessible to seventeenth-century Anglicans.

Herbert's description of the home and household of the priest also has a quasi-monastic quality. Yet its purpose is not to be seen in isolation. It is to be 'a copy and model for his parish' (Chapter X). The priest studies, prays and works within the framework of a community life both within the household and within the wider parish. The priest is to be someone of learning. Although the most vital learning is spiritual rather than intellectual, it is clear from all the references in *The Country Parson* that the house is, like a good Benedictine monastery, to have a well-stocked library. Herbert expected all the members of the priest's home to share, to some degree, in the ministry. So 'home' is a place where the Christian life is lived with some intensity and, as the poem 'The Family' makes clear, home is also where God dwells.

Household
Readings

1 *The Country Parson*, Chapter X
2 The Family

1

The Country Parson, Chapter X
The Parson in his House

The Parson is very exact in the governing of his house, making it a copy and model for his parish. He knows the temper and pulse of every person in his house, and accordingly either meets with their vices or advanceth their virtues. His wife is either religious, or night and day he is winning her to it. Instead of the qualities of the world, he requires only three of her: first, a training up of her children and maids in the fear of God, with prayers, and catechizing, and all religious duties. Secondly, a curing and healing of all wounds and sores with her own hands, which skill either she brought with her, or he takes care she shall learn it of some religious neighbour. Thirdly, a providing for her family in such sort as that neither they want a competent sustenation nor her husband be brought in debt. His children he first makes Christians, and then commonwealth's men: the one he owes to his heavenly country, the other to his earthly, having no title to either, except he do good to both. Therefore, having seasoned them with all piety, not only words in praying and reading, but in actions, in visiting other sick children, and tending their wounds, and sending his charity by them to the poor, and sometimes giving them a little money to do it of themselves, that they get a delight in it, and enter favour with God, who weighs even children's actions, *I Kings* 14: 12, 13. He afterwards turns his care to fit all their dispositions with some calling, not sparing the eldest, but giving him the prerogative of his father's profession, which happily for his other children he is not able to do. Yet in binding them prentices (in case he think fit to do so) he takes care not to put them into vain trades, and unbefitting the reverence of their father's calling, such as are taverns for men, and lace-making for women; because those trades, for the most part, serve but the vices and vanities of the world, which he is to deny and not augment. However, he resolves with himself never to omit any present good deed of charity in consideration of providing a stock for his children, but assures himself that money thus lent to God is placed surer for his children's advantage than if it were given to the Chamber of London. Good deeds and good breeding are his two great stocks for his children; if God give anything above those, and not spent in them, he blesseth God, and lays it out as he sees cause. His servants are all religious, and were it not his duty to have them so, it were his profit, for none are so well served as by religious servants, both because they do best and because what they do is blessed and prospers. After religion, he teacheth them that three things make a complete servant – truth, and diligence, and neatness or cleanliness. Those that can read are allowed times for it, and those that cannot are taught, for all in his house are either teachers or learners, or both, so that his family is a school of religion, and they all account that to teach the ignorant is the greatest alms. Even the walls are not idle, but something is written or painted there which may excite the reader to a thought of piety, espe-cially the 101 Psalm, which is expressed in a fair table, as being the rule of the family. And when they go abroad, his wife among her neighbours is the beginner of good discourses, his children among children, his servants among other servants, so that as in the house of those that are skilled in music all are musicians, so in the house of a preacher all are preachers. He suffers not a lie or equivocation by any means in his house, but counts it the art and secret of governing to preserve a direct-ness and open plainness in all things, so that all his house knows that there is no help for a fault done but confession. He *himself*, or his *wife*, takes account of sermons, and how every one profits, comparing this year with the last; and besides the common prayers of the family, he straightly requires of all to pray by themselves before they sleep at night and stir out in the morning, and knows what prayers they say, and till they have learned them makes them kneel by him, esteeming that this private praying is a more voluntary act in them than when they are called to others' prayers, and that which, when they leave the family, they carry with them. He keeps his servants between love and fear, according as he finds them, but generally he distributes it thus: to his children he shows more love then terror, to his servants more terror than love, but an old good servant boards a child. The furniture of his house is very plain, but clean, whole, and sweet, as sweet as his garden can make; for he hath no money for such things, charity being his only perfume, which deserves cost when he can spare it. His fare is plain and common, but wholesome; what he hath is little, but very good; it con-sisteth most of mutton, beef, and veal; if he adds any thing for a great day or a stranger, his garden or orchard supplies it, or his barn and back-side: he goes no further for any entertainment lest he go into the world, esteeming it absurd that he should exceed who teacheth others temperance. But those which his home produceth he refuseth not, as coming cheap and easy, and arising from the improvement of things which otherwise would be lost. Wherein he admires and imitates the wonderful providence and thrift of the great householder of the world; for there being two things which as they are, are unuseful to man, – the one for smallness, as crumbs and scattered corn and the like, the other for the foulness, as wash and dirt, and things thereinto fallen, – God hath provided creatures for both: for the first, poultry; for the second, swine. These save man the labour, and doing that which either he could not do or was not fit for him to do, by taking both sorts of food into them, do as it were dress and prepare both for man in themselves by growing themselves fit for his table. The parson in his house observes fasting days, and particularly, as Sunday is his day of joy, so Friday his day of humiliation, which he celebrates not only with abstinence of diet, but also of company, recreation, and all outward contentments, and besides, with confession of sins and all acts of mortification. Now fasting days contain a treble obligation: First, of eating less that day than on other days; secondly of eating no pleasing or over-nourishing things, as the Israelites did eat sour herbs; thirdly, of eating no flesh, which is but the determination of the second rule by authority to this particular. The two former obligations are much more essential to a true fast than the third and last, and fasting days were fully performed by keeping of the two former, had not authority interposed; so that to eat little, and that unpleasant, is the natural rule of fasting, although it be flesh. For since fasting in Scripture language is an afflicting of our souls, if a piece of dry flesh at my table be more unpleasant to me than some fish there, certainly to eat the flesh, and not the fish, is to keep the fasting day naturally. And it is observable that the prohibiting of flesh came from hot countries, where both flesh alone, and much more with wine, is apt to nourish more than in cold regions, and where flesh may be much better spared and with more safety than elsewhere, where both the people and the drink being cold and phlegmatic, the eating of flesh is an antidote to both. For it is certain that a weak stomach being pre-possessed with flesh shall much better brook and bear a draught of beer than if it had taken before either fish or roots, or such things, which will discover itself by spitting, and rheum, or phlegm. To conclude, the parson, if he be in full health, keeps the three obligations, eating fish or roots, and that for quantity little, for quality unpleasant. If his body be weak and obstructed, as most students are, he cannot keep the last obligation nor suffer others in his house that are so to keep it, but only the two former, which also in diseases of exinanition (as consumptions) must be broken, for meat was made for man, not man for meat. To all this may be added, not for emboldening the unruly, but for the comfort of the weak, that not only sickness breaks these obligations of fasting, but sickliness also. For it is as unnatural to do anything that leads me to a sickness to which I am inclined, as not to get out of that sickness, when I am in it, by any diet. One thing is evident, that an English body, and a student's body, are two great obstructed vessels, and there is nothing that is food, and not physic, which doth less obstruct then flesh moderately taken, as being immoderately taken it is exceeding obstructive. And obstructions are the cause of most diseases.

2

The Family

What doth this noise of thoughts within my heart,
  As if they had a part?
What do these loud complaints and puling fears,
  As if there were no rule or ears?

But, Lord, the house and family are thine,
  Though some of them repine.
Turn out these wranglers, which defile thy seat:
  For where thou dwellest all is neat.

First Peace and Silence all disputes control,
  Then Order plays the soul;
And giving all things their set forms and hours,
  Makes of wild woods sweet walks and bowers.

Humble Obedience near the door doth stand,
  Expecting a command:
Than whom in waiting nothing seems more slow,
  Nothing more quick when she doth go.

Joys oft are there, and griefs as oft as joys:
  But griefs without a noise:
Yet speak they louder than distemper'd fears.
  What is so shrill as silent tears?

This is thy house, with these it doth abound:
  And where these are not found,
Perhaps thou com'st sometimes, and for a day;
  But not to make a constant stay.

The Church

Another significant element of Herbert's sense of place was the church building. He had a very positive understanding of God's presence in the church. The use of the words 'Temple' and 'Church' in his great poetic collection works on several levels. The community of the Church is the Body of Christ and the individual soul is the Temple of the Holy Spirit. But alongside these the building itself is seen as a sacred place. The parish church is, like the Jewish Temple, a place of meeting between humans and God. Herbert describes the parish priest on entering the church 'humbly adoring and worshipping the invisible majesty and presence of Almighty God' (*The Country Parson*, Chapter VIII). Baptism takes place there 'in the presence of God and his saints' (Chapter XXII). In the poem 'Perirrhanterium' Herbert exhorts the reader to show special respect in a church building for it is God's house not just a human meeting place. 'God is more there, than thou: for thou art there/ Only by his permission.' Elsewhere he suggests that a godly person may well have a custom of dropping into church for a brief prayer. This is not superstition but reverence to God's house and an occasion to thank God for dwelling in our midst (Chapter XXXI).

The building and its furnishings all have significance and point us towards a life of holiness. Herbert's poems in *The Temple* are structured to suggest a journey from the outer 'Church Porch' (the first section, full of moral exhortation and preparation) into the 'Church' itself (the central section which includes the poems of greatest spiritual depth). In Herbert's way of seeing things, the actual arrangement of the church speaks not only of liturgical functions but also of a spirituality of journey and pilgrimage. Throughout the poems there is a scattering of brief references to the physical features of the building acting as a medium for spiritual encounters.

There are also poems dedicated to parts of the building. There is only space here to hint at a few examples of their spiritual message. The very first poem of the central section is 'The Altar'. This stands not only for the theological centrality of Christ's cross and passion but also for the central action of the community within the building, the Eucharist, which makes effective in the present the saving actions of Christ. However, Herbert's reflections suggest that the altar that really matters is the human heart. 'Church-monuments' uses the tombs and memorials in the building as a focus for meditation on the frailty of human life. 'The Church Lock and Key' reminds the reader that what shuts us out from God's presence is only our sinfulness and the lack of desire. The solidity of the stones and steps of 'The Church-floor' speak to Herbert of the qualities of patience, humility, confidence, love and charity. These virtues are the solid stones of human holiness but only because the divine architect builds 'so strong in a weak heart'. Finally, in 'The Windows', Herbert implies that the colours and light of windows themselves in 'this glorious and transcendent place' have the power to reveal God's story. Yet just as the colours are fixed in the glass when it is fired so God's life is, as it were, fixed and fired into the holy preacher and shines forth. Without this, a preacher's many words in the building are empty things that on their own 'vanish like a flaring thing'.

In a sense the particular visible expression of the Body of Christ to which Herbert gave his loyalty, the national Church, was also a sacred place. It was local and particular yet also, for Herbert, part of the universal Church Catholic. These sentiments are clearly expressed in Herbert's poem 'The British Church'. 'She on the hills' (Rome) 'wantonly/ Allureth all' with her 'painted shrines'. 'She in the valley' (Calvin's Geneva), on the contrary, was 'so shy/ Of dressing, that her hair doth lie/ About her ears'. The Church of England is for Herbert his 'dearest Mother'. Her way is the middle way: 'The mean, thy praise and glory is'.

Herbert's loyalty to the Church was expressed practically in his attitude to his bishop as spiritual father and to the diocese as the local Church. Herbert's vision of a priest was by no means free-wheeling or autonomous. The parson is to keep up with his neighbouring priests and to assist them with worship or pastoral care when appropriate. There is a strong sense of solidarity in Herbert's vision of the priesthood and a priest is always to welcome another priest into his house and to receive him as if he were the greatest of lords (*The Country Parson*, Chapter XIX).

Church
Readings

1 *The Country Parson*, Chapter VIII

2 The Altar

3 The Church-floor

4 The Windows

5 The British Church

The Country Parson, Chapter VIII
The Parson on Sundays

The Country Parson, as soon as he awakes on Sunday morning, presently falls to work, and seems to himself so as a market man is when
the market day comes, or a shopkeeper when customers use to come in.
His thoughts are full of making the best of the day, and contriving it to
his best gains. To this end, besides his ordinary prayers, he makes a peculiar one for a blessing on the exercises of the day. That nothing befall
him unworthy of that Majesty before which he is to present himself,
but that all may be done with reverence to his glory, and with edification to his flock, humbly beseeching his Master that how or whenever
he punish him, it may be not in his ministry; then he turns to request
for his people that the Lord would be pleased to sanctify them all, that
they may come with holy hearts and awful minds into the congregation, and that the good God would pardon all those who come with
less prepared hearts than they ought. This done, he sets himself to the
consideration of the duties of the day, and if there be any extraordinary
addition to the customary exercises, either from the time of the year,
or from the state, or from God by a child born, or dead, or any other
accident, he contrives how and in what manner to induce it to the best
advantage. Afterwards, when the hour calls, with his family attending
him, he goes to church, at his first entrance *humbly adoring and worshipping the invisible majesty and presence of Almighty God*, and blessing the people, either openly or to himself. Then having read Divine
Service twice fully, and preached in the morning, and catechized in the
afternoon, he thinks he hath in some measure, according to poor and
frail man, discharged the public duties of the congregation. The rest
of the day he spends either in reconciling neighbours that are at vari-
ance, or in visiting the sick, or in exhortations to some of his flock by
themselves, whom his sermons cannot or do not reach. And every one
is more awaked when we come and say, *Thou art the man*. This way
he finds exceeding useful and winning; and these exhortations he calls
his privy purse, even as princes have theirs, besides their public disburs-
ments. At night, he thinks it a very fit time, both suitable to the joy of
the day and without hindrance to public duties, either to entertain some
of his neighbours or to be entertained of them, where he takes occasion
to discourse *of such things as are both profitable and pleasant, and to*

*raise up their minds to apprehend God's good blessing to our Church
and state – that order is kept in the one, and peace in the other, without
disturbance or interruption of public divine offices.* As he opened the
day with prayer, so he closeth it, humbly beseeching the Almighty to
pardon and accept our poor services and to improve them, that we may
grow therein, and that our feet may be like hind's feet, ever climbing up
higher and higher unto him.

2

The Altar

A broken A L T A R, Lord, thy servant rears,
Made of a heart, and cemented with tears:
   Whose parts are as thy hand did frame;
   No workman's tool hath touch'd the same.
      A H E A R T a l o n e
      Is such a stone,
      As nothing but
      Thy pow'r doth cut.
      Wherefore each part
      Of my hard heart
      Meets in this frame,
      To praise thy name.
 That if I chance to hold my peace,
   These stones to praise thee may not cease.
O let thy blessed S A C R I F I C E be mine,
And sanctify this A L T A R to be thine.

3

The Church-floor

Mark you the floor? that square and speckled stone,
   Which looks so firm and strong,
     Is *Patience*:

And th' other black and grave, wherewith each one
   Is checker'd all along,
     Humility:

The gentle rising, which on either hand
  Leads to the Choir above,
    Is *Confidence*:

But the sweet cement, which in one sure band
  Ties the whole frame, is *Love*
    And *Charity*.

  Hither sometimes Sin steals, and stains
  The marble's neat and curious veins:
But all is cleansed when the marble weeps.
  Sometimes Death, puffing at the door,
  Blows all the dust about the floor:
But while he thinks to spoil the room, he sweeps.
  Blest be the *Architect*, whose art
  Could build so strong in a weak heart.

4

The Windows

Lord, how can man preach thy eternal word?
  He is a brittle crazy glass:
Yet in thy temple thou dost him afford
  This glorious and transcendent place,
  To be a window, through thy grace.

But when thou dost anneal in glass thy story,
  Making thy life to shine within
The holy Preacher's; then the light and glory
  More rev'rend grows, and more doth win:
  Which else show watrish, bleak, and thin.

Doctrine and life, colours and light, in one
  When they combine and mingle, bring
A strong regard and awe: but speech alone
  Doth vanish like a flaring thing,
  And in the ear, not conscience ring.

5

The British Church

I joy, dear Mother, when I view
Thy perfect lineaments, and hue
  Both sweet and bright.
Beauty in thee takes up her place,
And dates her letters from thy face,
  When she doth write.

A fine aspect in fit array,
Neither too mean, nor yet too gay,
  Shows who is best.
Outlandish looks may not compare:
For all they either painted are,
  Or else undrest.

She on the hills, which wantonly
Allureth all, in hope to be
  By her preferr'd,
Hath kiss'd so long her painted shrines,
That ev'n her face by kissing shines,
  For her reward.

She in the valley is so shy
Of dressing, that her hair doth lie
  About her ears:
While she avoids her neighbour's pride,
She wholly goes on th' other side,
  And nothing wears.

But dearest Mother, what those miss,
The mean, thy praise and glory is,
  And long may be.
Blessed be God, whose love it was
To double-moat thee with his grace,
  And none but thee.

The Village

For Herbert, the priest is always a person in a specific place, the parish. The parish is both a religious and a social reality. It is the community of all people who dwell in a particular place however infrequently they darken the doors of the church building (*The Country Parson*, Chapter XIX). Certainly in Herbert's time and even until today in a few English rural places, the parish defined who you were. It dominated other human associations. It was the one place that you belonged to from birth to death – and even beyond death. Your ancestors' graves filled the churchyard and you might expect to be buried next to them in your turn. This sense of place was intense, shaped as it was by landscape as well as social or religious ties.

In our own more urbanized, mobile and perhaps rootless culture, this vision appears to some people to offer a security that many of us lack. There may be some truth in this feeling but the results of parochialism could also be stifling. There are hints of this in Herbert when he suggests that the priest should try to encourage parishioners to have a sense of the wider Church and civic society and to honour their obligations of charity to neighbouring parishes. Herbert uses the place word 'neighbourhood' to describe the attitude of neighbourliness that he sees as a duty and debt.

It is by being located in such specific places that the priest has an identity and a role. The priest's attitude is to view the parish as his own family (*The Country Parson*, Chapter XVI) and 'all his joy and thought' (Chapter XVII). He has an immense sense of responsibility for the local community because he 'is in God's stead to his parish' (Chapter XX).

For Herbert, this vision of a priest in a place is expressed most commonly in a pattern of daily visiting around the village which he describes in *The Country Parson* as 'the parson in circuit' (Chapter XIV). The priest is to be present to people 'most naturally as they are'. There is an intensity of presence in Herbert's description of the priest's life and ministry that may feel oppressive from a contemporary point of view. However, it is important to recall that the problem of non-resident clergy had been an issue in the English Church since the Middle Ages and continued to be so even after the formation of a reformed Church of England. So 'residence' became an important ideal in any agenda for a reformed and more spiritually alert clergy. As a consequence Herbert's parson essentially commits himself to his immediate locality and only journeys outside his normal place for 'a just occasion (which he diligently and strictly weigheth)'. There is a spiritual discipline involved in not continually seeking to escape being alongside the people a priest is called to serve.

Village
Reading

1 *The Country Parson*, Chapter XIV

I

The Country Parson, Chapter XIV
The Parson in Circuit

The Country Parson upon the afternoons in the week-days takes occasion sometimes to visit in person, now one quarter of his parish, now another. For there he shall find his flock most naturally as they are, wallowing in the midst of their affairs; whereas on Sunday it is easy for them to compose themselves to order, which they put on as their holy-day clothes, and come to church in frame, but commonly the next day put off both. When he comes to any house, first he blesseth it, and then as he finds the persons of the house employed, so he forms his discourse. Those that he finds religiously employed he both commends them much, and furthers them when he is gone in their employment; as if he finds them reading, he furnisheth them with good books; if curing poor people, he supplies them with receipts, and instructs them further in that skill, showing them how acceptable such works are to God, and wishing them ever to do the cures with their own hands, and not to put them over to servants. Those that he finds busy in the works of their calling, he commendeth them also; for it is a good and just thing for every one to do their own business. But then he admonisheth them of two things: first, that they dive not too deep into worldly affairs, plunging themselves over head and ears into carking and caring; but that they so labour as neither to labour anxiously, nor distrustfully, nor profanely. Then they labour anxiously, when they overdo it, to the loss of their quiet and health; then distrustfully, when they doubt

God's providence, thinking that their own labour is the cause of their thriving, as if it were in their own hands to thrive or not to thrive. *Then they labour profanely, when they set themselves to work like brute beasts, never raising their thoughts to God, nor sanctifying their labour with daily prayer; when on the Lord's day they do unnecessary servile work, or in time of divine service on other holy days, except in the cases of extreme poverty, and in the seasons of seedtime and harvest.* Secondly, he adviseth them so to labour for wealth and maintenance as that they make not that the end of their labour, but that they may have wherewithal to serve God the better, and to do good deeds. After these discourses, if they be poor and needy whom he thus finds labouring, he gives them somewhat; and opens not only his mouth, but his purse to their relief, that so they go on more cheerfully in their vocation, and himself be ever the more welcome to them. Those that the parson finds idle or ill employed he chides not at first, for that were neither civil nor profitable, but always in the close, before he departs from them; yet in this he distinguisheth; for if he be a plain countryman he reproves him plainly, for they are not sensible of fineness; if they be of higher quality they commonly are quick, and sensible, and very tender of reproof; and therefore he lays his discourse so that he comes to the point very leisurely, and oftentimes, as Nathan did, in the person of another, making them to reprove themselves. However, one way or other, he ever reproves them, that he may keep himself pure, and not be entangled in others' sins. Neither in this doth he forbear, though there be company by; for as when the offence is particular, and against me, I am to follow our Saviour's rule, and to take my brother aside and reprove him; so when the offence is public and against God, I am then to follow the Apostle's rule, *I Timothy* 5: 20, and to *rebuke openly* that which is done openly. Besides these occasional discourses, the parson questions what order is kept in the house, as about prayers morning and evening on their knees, reading of Scripture, catechizing, singing of psalms at their work and on holy days; who can read, who not; and sometimes he hears the children read himself, and blesseth them, encouraging also the servants to learn to read, and offering to have them taught on holy days by his servants. If the parson were ashamed of particularizing in these things he were not fit to be a parson; but he holds the rule that nothing is little in God's service: if it once have the honour of that name, it grows great instantly. Wherefore neither disdaineth he to enter into the poorest cottage, though he even creep into it, and though it smell never so loathsomely; for both God is there also, and those for whom

God died. And so much the rather doth he so, as his access to the poor is more comfortable than to the rich, and in regard of himself it is more humiliation. These are the parson's general aims in his circuit; but with these he mingles other discourses for conversation sake, and to make his higher purposes slip the more easily.

Nation and World

Nevertheless, George Herbert has a sense of place beyond the local parish or diocese and neighbourhood. Herbert is typical of his time in having a strong sense of service to his country. The parish implies both church community and village. Herbert's understanding of 'nation' also involves an overlap of Church and society. His priest is to bring up his children first as Christians and second as 'commonwealth's men' (*sic*). When he invites his neighbours to a meal he is to 'raise up their minds to apprehend God's good blessing to our Church and state' (*The Country Parson*, Chapter VIII).

Although Herbert's criticism of idleness has a moral tone, in the longest section on service it also refers to the debt that each person owed to their country (Chapter XXXII). This service may be local or national. Thus the person who has some spare time and energy left after normal employment and care for the family should think of taking on some public role in the locality, such as managing the woods or common land. People with 'gravity and ripeness of judgement' should consider putting themselves forwards as lay magistrates (Justices of the Peace). Herbert also suggests that to become a Member of Parliament, and to be conscientious and active there, is one of the highest duties a person can undertake for the sake of the nation. Or one might become an expert in fortification or navigation. A life in commerce is not to be sneered at, especially for younger sons who might otherwise spend their days 'in dressing, complimenting, visiting, and sporting'. Finally Herbert suggests that foreign travel was of value but even here service of one's country is the main motivation. The traveller might either learn business and manufacturing skills in Europe that could be brought home or might think of serving in the new colonies in America which Herbert clearly sees as a religious as well as a civil occupation.

For the modern reader, Herbert's portrayal of an overlap between Church and society, or Church and nation, raises obvious problems. Herbert accepts the notion of religious and social Establishment without questioning it. Many Christians these days would reject or at least seriously criticize this. Indeed, if we compare the writings of George Herbert with those of Thomas Traherne or Henry Vaughan only a few decades later, it is clear that after the terrible divisions of the Civil War Herbert's ideal of a well-ordered Church connected to a well-ordered nation was no longer easy to sustain. In contrast to Herbert, both Traherne and

Vaughan, while faithful members of the Church of England, describe a much more inward, mystical, non-institutional spirituality.

Despite these difficulties, in other ways George Herbert's vision of an overlap of Church and civil society does have positive qualities that continue to resonate with contemporary spiritual values. For one thing, this overlap is a reminder that a holistic spirituality should be neither individualistic nor spiritualized. It necessarily has a social, public or civil dimension. The overlap also emphasizes a more inclusive model of the Church and of belonging (by virtue of being born into a given locality) in contrast to a more purified, gathered and therefore elitist model. Equally, Herbert reminds Christians of all ages that a sense of place can become decidedly parochial. In his own modest way, Herbert points to horizons beyond the local – whether this is other communities nearby with whom his parishioners might share their abundance in a time of trial or need or whether it be service of the country and society at large. In the twenty-first century, approaches to spirituality rightly emphasize a more global sense of place and community than Herbert would have understood. Yet Herbert's emphasis on the importance of locality, of the *local*, paradoxically speaks to a contemporary need in the West to recover a sense of the small scale and the personal in a world that increasingly operates on a macro and impersonal level.

Nation and World
Reading

1 *The Country Parson*, Chapter XXXII

I

The Country Parson, Chapter XXXII
The Parson's Surveys

The Country Parson hath not only taken a particular survey of the faults of his own parish, but a general also of the diseases of the time, that so, when his occasions carry him abroad, or bring strangers to him, he may be the better armed to encounter them. The great and national sin of this land he esteems to be idleness, great in itself and great in consequence; for when men have nothing to do, then they fall to drink, to steal, to whore, to scoff, to revile, to all sorts of gamings. Come, they say, we have nothing to do, let's go to the tavern, or to the stews, or what not. Wherefore the parson strongly opposeth this sin wheresoever he goes. And because idleness is twofold, the one having no calling, the other in walking carelessly in our calling, he first represents to everybody the necessity of a vocation. The reason of this assertion is taken from the nature of man, wherein God hath placed two great instruments, reason in the soul and a hand in the body, as engagements of working, so that even in Paradise man had a calling, and how much more out of Paradise, when the evils which he is now subject unto may be prevented or diverted by reasonable employment. Besides, every gift or ability is a talent to be accounted for, and to be improved to our Master's advantage. Yet it is also a debt to our country to have a calling, and it concerns the commonwealth that none should be idle, but all busied. Lastly, riches are the blessing of God, and the great instrument of doing admirable good; therefore all are to procure them honestly and seasonably when they are not better employed. Now this reason crosseth not our Saviour's precept of selling what we have, because when we have sold all, and given it to the poor, we must not be idle, but labour to get more, that we may give more, according to St. Paul's rule, *Ephesians* 4: 28. *I Thessalonians* 4: 11, 12. So that our Saviour's selling is so far from crossing St. Paul's working that it rather establisheth it, since they that have nothing are fittest to work. Now, because the only opposer to this doctrine is the gallant, who is witty enough to abuse both others and himself, and who is ready to ask if he shall mend shoes, or what he shall do? Therefore, the parson, unmoved, showeth that *ingenuous and fit* employment is never wanting to those that seek it. But if it should be, the assertion stands thus: All are either to have a calling, or prepare for it; he that hath or can have yet no employment, if he truly and seriously prepare for it, he is safe and within bounds. Wherefore all are either presently to enter into a calling, if they be fit for it and it for them, or else to examine with care, and advice, what they are fittest for, and to prepare for that with all diligence. But it will not be amiss in this exceeding useful point to descend to particulars, for exactness lies in particulars. Men are either single or married. The married and housekeeper hath his hands full if he do what he ought to do. For there are two branches of his affairs: first, the improvement of his family, by bringing them up in the fear and nurture of the Lord; and secondly, the improvement of his grounds, by drowning, or draining, or stocking, or fencing and ordering his land to the best advantage both of himself and his neighbours. The Italian says, none fouls his hands in his own business and it is an honest and just care so it exceed not bounds, for every one to employ himself to the advancement of his affairs, that he may have wherewithal to do good. But his family is his best care, to labour Christian souls, and raise them to their height, even to heaven; to dress and prune them, and take as much joy in a straight-growing child or servant as a gardener doth in a choice tree. Could men find out this delight, they would seldom be from home, whereas now of any place they are least there. But if after all this care well dispatched the housekeeper's family be so small, and his dexterity so great, that he have leisure to look out, the village or parish which either he lives in, or is near unto it, is his employment. He considers every one there, and either helps them in particular or hath general propositions to the whole town or hamlet, of advancing the public stock, and managing commons or woods, according as the place suggests. But if he may be of the commission of peace, there is nothing to that: no commonwealth in the world hath a braver institution than that of justices of the peace, for it is both a security to the king, who hath so many dispersed officers at his beck throughout the kingdom accountable for the public good, and also an honourable employment of a gentle or nobleman in the country he lives in, enabling him with power to do good, and to restrain all those who else might both trouble him and the whole state. Wherefore it behoves all who are come to the gravity and ripeness of judgment for so excellent a place, not to refuse, but rather to procure it. And whereas there are usually three objections made against the place: the one, the abuse of it, by taking petty country bribes; the other, the casting of it on mean persons, especially in some shires; and lastly, the trouble of it, these are so far from deterring any good men from the place, that they kindle them rather to redeem the dignity either from true faults or unjust aspersions. Now, for single men, they are either heirs or younger brothers; the heirs are to prepare in all the forementioned points against the time of their practice. Therefore they are to mark their father's discretion in ordering his house and affairs, and also elsewhere when they see any remarkable point of education or good husbandry, and to transplant it in time to his own home, with the same care as others, when they meet with good fruit, get a graft of the tree, enriching their orchard and neglecting their house. Besides, they are to read books of law and justice, especially, the statutes at large. As for better books of divinity, they are not in this consideration, because we are about a calling and a preparation thereunto. But chiefly and above all things they are to frequent sessions and sizes, for it is both an honour which they owe to the reverend judges and magistrates to attend them at least in their shire, and it is a great advantage to know the practice of the land, for our law is practice. Sometimes he may go to court, as the eminent place both of good and ill. At other times he is to travel over the king's dominions, cutting out the kingdom into portions, which every year he surveys piecemeal. When there is a parliament, he is to endeavour by all means to be a knight or burgess there, for there is no school to a parliament. And when he is there he must not only be a morning man, but at committees also, for there the particulars are exactly discussed which are brought from thence to the House but in general. When none of these occasions call him abroad, every morning that he is at home he must either ride the great horse or exercise some of his military gestures. For all gentlemen that are now weakened and disarmed with sedentary lives are to know the use of their arms; and as the husbandman labours for them, so must they fight for and defend them when occasion calls. This is the duty of each to other, which they ought to fulfil. And the parson is a lover of and exciter to justice in all things, even as John the Baptist squared out to every one (even to soldiers) what to do. As for younger brothers, those whom the parson finds loose, and not engaged in some profession by their parents, whose neglect in this point is intolerable, and a shameful wrong both to the commonwealth and their own house; to them, after he hath showed the unlawfulness of spending the day in dressing, complimenting, visiting, and sporting, he first commends the study of the civil law, as a brave and wise knowledge, the professors whereof were much employed by Queen Elizabeth, because it is the key of commerce, and discovers the rules of foreign nations. Secondly, he commends the mathematics as the only wonderworking knowledge, and therefore requiring the best spirits. After the several knowledge of these, he adviseth to insist and dwell chiefly on the two noble branches thereof, of fortification and navigation; the one being useful to all countries, and the other especially to islands. But if the young gallant think these courses dull and phlegmatic, where can he busy himself better than in those new plantations and discoveries, which are not only a noble, but also, as they may be handled, a religious employment? Or let him travel into Germany and France, and observing the artifices and manufactures there, transplant them hither, as divers have done lately, to our country's advantage.

5

Discipleship and Inner Struggle

One of the most important threads running through Herbert's poems is a personal relationship with God characterized by struggle both on the part of God and on that of the human heart. The intensity of the poems suggests that the struggle they describe was a real and personal one rather than something merely contrived, although it has already been indicated that their purpose was not autobiographical but to evoke a deepening of the reader's own relationship with God. The words quoted by Isaak Walton from a message accompanying his poetic writings that Herbert allegedly sent from his deathbed to his friend Nicholas Ferrar accord well with the substance of the poems themselves. The message suggested that the poems were 'a picture of the many spiritual conflicts that have passed betwixt God and my soul before I could subject mine to the will of Jesus my Master: in whose service I have now found perfect freedom'.

The poems themselves, however, do not chart a simple spiritual path, for example the classical progression from purgative way to unitive way or some equivalent. Complexity and simplicity, doubt and faith vie with each other throughout. Even the final poem of the central section of *The Temple*, 'Love (3)', continues to express a deep spiritual struggle. Despite the apparent resolution and surrender expressed in its last line, there is an ambiguity that suggests that such surrenders are never finally conclusive on this side of death. It is only the latest of several such surrenders throughout the poems. In fact, the poems of the middle section of *The Temple*, as a whole, chart a fluctuating relationship with God in which God struggles with Herbert's 'peevish heart' ('Sion', line 13).

Inner Struggle

It is impossible to focus the nature of Herbert's inner struggle towards
spiritual freedom on a single key theme. Structurally, the poems seem
to offer a sense of movement from a more moral, active, meditative
stance in 'The Church Porch', the first section of *The Temple*, to a
more God-centred, contemplative and passive mood at the end of 'The
Church'. However, if there is indeed a movement towards contemplative experience it also involves more complex spiritual movements.
Herbert's theology of the human person suggests that humanity is
both the meeting place of heaven and earth and a place of conflict,
'A wonder tortur'd in the space/ Betwixt this world and that of grace'
('Affliction (4)').

It is fair to summarize Herbert's struggle as the quest for assurance
(see his poem 'Assurance') and a battle to accept God's love, but this
covers a variety of sub-plots. Herbert's basic problem initially appears
simply as the classically Protestant sense of unworthiness and inability
to cope with the single-mindedness of God's love. On further reflection, however, pride is also clearly part of Herbert's struggle. Even in
that final poem, 'Love (3)', Herbert shows every sign of wanting to be
worthy, to merit God's love. What is lacking at Love's feast? 'A guest,
I answer'd, worthy to be here.' The fundamental question throughout
the central section of *The Temple* is how the writer is to allow God to
love and serve him. How is Herbert to surrender his own standards?
This is a subtle form of pride but pride nonetheless. It seems good to be
worthy and to desire to be worthy. However, in reality that is to place
the human capacity to respond to God at the heart of the matter rather
than God's free gift of love. Herbert does not deny that we are called
to respond to God but the response is, paradoxically, to accept our inability to offer true love in return for true love.

It would be strange if Herbert's aristocratic sensibilities had no further impact after his conversion. It is one thing to renounce a career
in public life and quite another to accept the full consequences. A
number of poems express frustration and the temptation to give up.
'Affliction (1)' suggests that the writer can see no sense in what is hap-
pening in his relationship with God. 'Well, I will change the service,
and go seek/ Some other master out.' As if to underline that there is
no simple progression in the human spiritual pilgrimage, a much later
poem, 'The Collar', has similar sentiments. 'I struck the board, and

cry'd, No more./ I will abroad./ What? shall I ever sigh and pine?' The poem's dramatic form indicates the continuing temptation to rebellion. Herbert seems to be raging against his own imperfections but behind this lies a degree of self-serving. The initial response is not surrender but revolt against the ultimate renunciation of self that seems to be required.

The endings of both 'Affliction' and 'The Collar' suggest that nothing more is asked of humans than a simple acceptance of God's love. This battle to accept that God is love rather than simply a judge is another dimension of Herbert's struggle. God confounds reasonable expectations. Humans are sinners and utterly unworthy; logically they should be condemned. No doubt the poem 'Justice (2)' expresses a contrast both between the Old Law and the New Law of Christ and between the New Law and Herbert's own experience. The point is that fear belongs to the past. It is broadly true that Herbert does not appear to battle with an existential fear of God even while he struggles to accept that God *ought* not to be feared.

Herbert's struggle with God and the movement towards spiritual freedom is just as real as it is, in a somewhat different guise, in Catholic Reformation writings such as those of Ignatius Loyola. Although the will of God is central to Herbert, the dominant image for God's way of being and acting is Love. The spiritual dynamic, therefore, cannot be one of salvation simply *imposed* on human beings from outside rather than operating from within their lives and experience. God's love is conclusively and freely offered. It is not provisionally on offer depending on the human capacity to earn it. After Christ, there is nothing more to be achieved or completed in salvation. Such a view is equally true of the Protestant Herbert and the Catholic Ignatius Loyola. Yet, equally, both recognize that God's love has to be truly received.

In the poem 'Redemption' Herbert employs the imagery of tenants and leases. The poet as tenant seeks to 'make a suit' to God in heaven who is the 'rich Lord' requesting that he be given a new lease as the old was no longer satisfactory. When he finds his Lord it is not in heaven but strangely on earth amidst thieves and murderers. The suit is immediately granted on sight without more discussion. This conclusion has sometimes been read as indicating that the human search for God is ultimately meaningless from the point of view of Reformed theology. However, this would mistake the poem's inner dynamism. The central point of the poem is not that seeking God is valueless but that God in

Christ is not to be found in the expected place. The writer 'knowing his great birth' sought God 'in great resorts;/ In cities, theatres, gardens, parks and courts'. In fact God is found among the unworthy and powerless. This provides a salutary lesson to the poet who, it seems, struggles with such a notion. God grants the suit from within the messiness of the human condition, not from the safety of power and invulnerability.

Thus it is the case in 'Redemption', as it is in the poem 'Love (3)', that nothing is imposed but everything is granted. God is revealed as the one who respects the human person. The final surrender of the poet in 'Love' ('You must sit down, says Love, and taste my meat:/ So I did sit and eat') is neither hopeless resignation nor the act of someone who obeys an order. It is the acceptance of an invitation. In that acceptance is freedom. This is because it involves, too, the realization that in the invitation to eat Love's meat 'I the unkind, ungrateful' have been granted a true vision of real value before God.

Struggle
Readings

1 Assurance

2 Love (3)

3 Affliction (1)

4 The Collar

5 Redemption

1

Assurance

O spiteful bitter thought!
Bitterly spiteful thought! Couldst thou invent
So high a torture? Is such poison bought?
Doubtless, but in the way of punishment,
  When wit contrives to meet with thee,
  No such rank poison can there be.

Thou said'st but even now,
That all was not so fair, as I conceiv'd,
Betwixt my God and me; that I allow
And coin large hopes; but, that I was deceiv'd:
    Either the league was broke, or near it;
    And, that I had great cause to fear it.

And what to this? what more
Could poison, if it had a tongue, express?
What is thy aim? wouldst thou unlock the door
To cold despairs, and gnawing pensiveness?
    Wouldst thou raise devils? I see, I know
    I writ thy purpose long ago.

But I will to my Father,
Who heard thee say it. O most gracious Lord,
If all the hope and comfort that I gather,
Were from my self, I had not half a word,
    Not half a letter to oppose
    What is objected by my foes.

But thou art my desert:
And in this league, which now my foes invade,
Thou art not only to perform thy part,
But also mine; as when the league was made
    Thou didst at once thy self indite,
    And hold my hand, while I did write.

Wherefore if thou canst fail,
Then can thy truth and I: but while rocks stand,
And rivers stir, thou canst not shrink or quail:
Yea, when both rocks and all things shall disband,
    Then shalt thou be my rock and tower,
    And make their ruin praise thy power.

Now foolish thought go on,
Spin out thy thread, and make thereof a coat
To hide thy shame: for thou hast cast a bone
Which bounds on thee, and will not down thy throat:
    What for it self love once began,
    Now love and truth will end in man.

2

Love (3)

Love bade me welcome: yet my soul drew back,
    Guilty of dust and sin.
But quick-ey'd Love, observing me grow slack
    From my first entrance in,
Drew nearer to me, sweetly questioning,
    If I lack'd anything.

A guest, I answer'd, worthy to be here:
    Love said, you shall be he.
I the unkind, ungrateful? Ah my dear,
    I cannot look on thee.
Love took my hand, and smiling did reply,
    Who made the eyes but I?

Truth Lord, but I have marr'd them: let my shame
    Go where it doth deserve.
And know you not, says Love, who bore the blame?
    My dear, then I will serve.
You must sit down, says Love, and taste my meat:
    So I did sit and eat.

3

Affliction (1)

When first thou didst entice to thee my heart
    I thought the service brave:
So many joys I writ down for my part,
    Besides what I might have
Out of my stock of natural delights,
Augmented with thy gracious benefits.

I looked on thy furniture so fine,
    And made it fine to me:
Thy glorious household-stuff did me entwine,
    And 'tice me unto thee.
Such stars I counted mine: both heav'n and earth
Paid me my wages in a world of mirth.

What pleasures could I want, whose King I served?
  Where joys my fellows were?
Thus argu'd into hopes, my thoughts reserved
  No place for grief or fear.
Therefore my sudden soul caught at the place,
And made her youth and fierceness seek thy face.

At first thou gav'st me milk and sweetnesses;
  I had my wish and way:
My days were straw'd with flow'rs and happiness;
  There was no month but May.
But with my years sorrow did twist and grow,
And made a party unawares for woe.

My flesh began unto my soul in pain,
  Sicknesses cleave my bones;
Consuming agues dwell in ev'ry vein,
  And tune my breath to groans.
Sorrow was all my soul; I scarce believed,
Till grief did tell me roundly, that I lived.

When I got health, thou took'st away my life,
  And more; for my friends die:
My mirth and edge was lost; a blunted knife
  Was of more use than I.
Thus thin and lean without a fence or friend,
I was blown through with ev'ry storm and wind.

Whereas my birth and spirit rather took
  The way that takes the town;
Thou didst betray me to a lingring book,
  And wrap me in a gown.
I was entangled in the world of strife,
Before I had the power to change my life.

Yet, for I threatned oft the siege to raise,
  Not simpring all mine age,
Thou often didst with Academic praise
  Melt and dissolve my rage.
I took thy sweetned pill, till I came where
I could not go away, nor persevere.

Yet lest perchance I should too happy be
   In my unhappiness,
Turning my purge to food, thou throwest me
   Into more sicknesses.
Thus doth thy power cross-bias me, not making
Thine own gift good, yet me from my ways taking.

Now I am here, what thou wilt do with me
   None of my books will show:
I read, and sigh, and wish I were a tree;
   For sure I then should grow
To fruit or shade: at least some bird would trust
Her household to me, and I should be just.

Yet, though thou troublest me, I must be meek;
   In weakness must be stout.
Well, I will change the service, and go seek
   Some other master out.
Ah my dear God! though I am clean forgot,
Let me not love thee, if I love thee not.

4

The Collar

I struck the board, and cry'd, No more.
   I will abroad.
What? shall I ever sigh and pine?
My lines and life are free; free as the road,
   Loose as the wind, as large as store.
     Shall I be still in suit?
   Have I no harvest but a thorn
   To let me blood, and not restore
What I have lost with cordial fruit?
     Sure there was wine
   Before my sighs did dry it: there was corn
    Before my tears did drown it.
   Is the year only lost to me?
    Have I no bays to crown it?
No flowers, no garlands gay? all blasted?
    All wasted?

Not so, my heart: but there is fruit,
    And thou hast hands.

Recover all thy sigh-blown age
On double pleasures: leave thy cold dispute
Of what is fit, and not; forsake thy cage,
        Thy rope of sands,
Which petty thoughts have made, and made to thee
    Good cable, to enforce and draw,
            And be thy law,
    While thou didst wink and wouldst not see.
            Away; take heed:
            I will abroad.
Call in thy death's head there: tie up thy fears.
            He that forbears
        To suit and serve his need,
            Deserves his load.
But as I rav'd and grew more fierce and wild
            At every word,
Me thoughts I heard one calling, *Child*:
            And I reply'd, *My Lord*.

5

Redemption

Having been tenant long to a rich Lord,
    Not thriving, I resolved to be bold,
    And make a suit unto him, to afford
A new small-rented lease, and cancel th' old.
In heaven at his manor I him sought:
    They told me there, that he was lately gone
    About some land, which he had dearly bought
Long since on earth, to take possession.
I straight return'd, and knowing his great birth,
    Sought him accordingly in great resorts;
    In cities, theatres, gardens, parks and courts:
At length I heard a ragged noise and mirth
    Of thieves and murderers: there I him espied
    Who straight, *Your suit is granted,* said, and died.

The Calling of Discipleship: A Holy Life

For Herbert, there is a close link between the demands of discipleship and Christian service and between service and personal holiness.
Nowhere is this made more explicit than in his treatise *The Country
Parson*. Although this treatise is apparently limited to the life of the
priest, it may usefully be reread in terms of Christian ministry more
broadly. Equally, it is not difficult to see that the fundamental spiritual
values that are portrayed are, with few exceptions, actually those of
Christian discipleship in the most inclusive sense.

There is a totality to Herbert's portrayal of the priest. His emphasis on personal holiness serves to underline that to be a pastor is not
merely a job but a way of life. It involves every moment and every
aspect of life including how the priest spends money or takes leisure
(Chapter III), behaves courteously, gives charitably or offers hospitality
(Chapters XI & XII) and even how he manages his own household and
family (Chapter X). To be effective in pastoral service involves considerable spiritual struggle (Chapter XXXIII) and Herbert's ideal pastor
continually strives to become 'an absolute master and commander of
himself, for all the purposes which God hath ordained him' (Chapter
III). Yet, despite Herbert's rather traditional emphasis on mortification, he is quite clear that it is more important to observe the spirit
rather than purely the letter of ascetical practices such as fasting. This is
particularly true if the person is physically weak (Chapter X). Perhaps
Herbert's sensitivity refers to his own experience of poor health which
had led him while a student at Cambridge to be forced to supplement
the traditional Lenten fare.

Herbert recommended that the parson should be fed by intellectual pursuits. 'The country parson hath read the Fathers also, and the
schoolmen and the later writers, or a good proportion of all' (Chapter
V). Yet at the heart of the parson's pastoral ministry lies holiness. Without this nothing counts. So 'The Parson's Library' (Chapter XXXIII)
does not in fact refer to a collection of books but to a holy life.

The priest's eloquence as a preacher consists not so much in verbal
dexterity as in holiness in the sense of a personal and transformative engagement with God's scriptural Word. Herbert's parson is effective as
a preacher to the degree that his life is a window through which God's
grace can shine onto the community ('The Windows').

Herbert's view of the holiness of the minister or priest is somewhat ambiguous. In general, a thoroughly Protestant viewpoint tended to reject the medieval hierarchy of vocations – and especially the notion of a special priestly caste. However, in its search for balance, the Elizabethan Settlement had left the Church of England with significant elements of the older model of a distinctive priesthood.

Herbert stressed the vocational nature of every human life under God. His country parson is to respect and nurture the vocation of everyone. From the time of creation, all human beings have had a calling and that continues to remain true. 'All are either to have a calling, or prepare for it' (Chapter XXXII). The parson is not to despise the holiness of the lowliest of people or the most ordinary of places. 'He holds the rule that nothing is little in God's service: if it once have the honour of that Name, it grows great instantly' (*The Country Parson*, Chapter XIV).

Yet, alongside an emphasis on the common Christian calling, Herbert also retained a view of the particularity of the priesthood. Article XXXII of the 1562 Articles of Religion made it clear that clergy might equally marry or remain single 'at their own discretion'. Although the meaning of clerical celibacy varies according to historical context, it is the case that celibacy stands for a great deal more than mere sexual abstinence. A wider spirituality of lifestyle is implied by that particular boundary. Herbert's personal view of the best possible lifestyle for the priest seems to have been somewhat more tightly drawn. He allows that, for pragmatic reasons, it may be best for the priest to marry, yet 'The Country Parson, considering that virginity is a higher state than matrimony, and that the ministry requires the best and highest things, is rather unmarried than married' (Chapter IX). Interestingly, this somewhat unreformed aspect of Herbert's idealized portrait of the priest is rarely if ever commented upon. The apparent preference of Queen Elizabeth I for a celibate clergy at the time of the religious Settlement appears to have sustained sympathy for this viewpoint in parts of the Church of England until the end of the Stuart era.

In his lengthy chapter on 'The Parson's State of Life' (Chapter IX), George Herbert also paints an ascetical portrait of the priest, whether celibate or married. 'He spends his days in fasting and prayer'. Indeed, Herbert recommends that the priest should go beyond the minimum required by Church law. The priest is to add 'some other days for fasting and hours for prayer'. Interestingly, it is to early desert asceticism that Herbert turns for inspiration. 'He [the priest] often readeth the lives of the primitive monks, hermits and virgins.'

Even if Herbert appears to retain something of an earlier view of the priesthood, this needs to be qualified. In the Church of England, priesthood did not exist in theological or spiritual isolation from a relationship to a specific community. The Church of England priesthood is not a substitute for the call to holiness of the whole community. Priesthood therefore has a more exemplary quality. Herbert would surely have understood his comments on celibacy and on the ascetic life of the priest to be a kind of lesson on the cost of discipleship offered to all baptized Christians.

Effectiveness and integrity in leading public worship was intimately connected to the pastor's own spiritual depths. For Herbert, there is a particular intimacy between God and those who preside at Holy Communion and this lays a considerable burden upon them (*The Country Parson*, Chapter XXII).

The priesthood is a 'Blest Order, which in power dost so excel' ('The Priesthood').

Yet the gap between this awesome calling and frail human nature, sin and failings, is vast. A person can only respond to the call to priesthood in full knowledge of unworthiness. The poem 'Aaron' plays with the imagery of dress, inward and outer, no doubt with half an eye on the controversy regarding the use of vestments. The true Aaron has 'Holiness on the head,/ Light and perfections on the breast'. Yet this is not so in the 'poor priest' (Herbert perhaps) who is by nature 'drest' in profaneness, defects and passions. The only answer to human unworthiness is to 'put on Christ' for 'In him I am well drest'.

A Holy Life
Readings

1 *The Country Parson*, Chapter III

2 *The Country Parson*, Chapter IX

3 The Priesthood

4 Aaron

I

The Country Parson, Chapter III
The Parson's Life

The Country Parson is exceeding exact in his Life, being holy, just, prudent, temperate, bold, grave, in all his ways. And because the two highest points of life, wherein a Christian is most seen, are patience and mortification: patience in regard of afflictions – mortification in regard of lusts and affections, and the stupefying and deading of all the clamorous powers of the soul; therefore he hath thoroughly studied these, that he may be an absolute master and commander of himself, for all the purposes which God hath ordained him. Yet in these points he labours most in those things which are most apt to scandalize his parish. And first, because country people live hardly, and therefore, as feeling their own sweat, and consequently knowing the price of money, are offended much with any who by hard usage increase their travail, the country parson is very circumspect in avoiding all covetousness, neither being greedy to get, nor niggardly to keep, nor troubled to lose any worldly wealth; but in all his words and actions slighting and dis-esteeming it, even to a wondering that the world should so much value wealth, which, in the day of wrath, hath not one dram of comfort for us. Secondly, because luxury is a very visible sin, the parson is very careful to avoid all the kinds thereof, but especially that of drinking, because it is the most popular vice; into which if he come, *he prostitutes himself* both to shame and sin, and by having *fellowship with the unfruitful works of darkness* he disableth himself of authority *to reprove them*; for sins make all equal whom they find together, and then they are worst who ought to be best. Neither is it for the servant of Christ to haunt inns, or taverns, or alehouses, *to the dishonour of his person and office*. The parson doth not so, but orders his life in such a fashion, that when death takes him, as the Jews and Judas did Christ, he may say as he did *I sat daily with you teaching in the Temple*. Thirdly, because country people (as indeed all honest men) do much esteem their word, it being the life of buying and selling and dealing in the world, therefore the parson is very strict in keeping his word, though it be to his own hindrance, as knowing that if he be not so, he will quickly be discovered and disregarded; neither will they believe him in the pulpit whom they cannot trust in his conversation. As for oaths and apparel, the disorders thereof are also very manifest. The parson's yea is yea, and nay, nay; and his apparel plain, but reverend and clean, without spots, or dust, or smell; the purity of his mind breaking out and dilating itself even to his body, clothes, and habitation.

2

The Country Parson, Chapter IX
The Parson's State of Life

The Country Parson, considering that virginity is a higher state than matrimony, and that the ministry requires the best and highest things, is rather unmarried than married. But yet as the temper of his body may be, or as the temper of his parish may be, where he may have occasion to converse with women, and that among suspicious men, *and other like circumstances considered*, he is rather married then unmarried. Let him communicate the thing often by prayer unto God, and as his grace shall direct him, so let him proceed. If he be unmarried and keep house, he hath not a woman in his house, but finds opportunities of having his meat dressed and other services done by men-servants at home, and his linen washed abroad. If he be unmarried, and sojourn, he never talks with any woman alone, but in the audience of others, and that seldom, and then also in a serious manner, never jestingly or sportfully. *He is very circumspect in all companies, both of his behaviour, speech, and very looks, knowing himself to be both suspected and envied. If he stand steadfast in his heart, having no necessity, but hath power over his own will, and hath so decreed in his heart that he will keep himself a virgin, he spends his days in fasting and prayer, and blesseth God for the gift of continency, knowing that it can no way be preserved but only by those means by which at first it was obtained. He therefore thinks it not enough for him to observe the fasting days of the Church, and the daily prayers enjoined him by authority, which he observeth out of humble conformity and obedience, but adds to them, out of choice and devotion, some other days for fasting and hours for prayers; and by these he keeps his body tame, serviceable, and healthful, and his soul fervent, active, young, and lusty as an eagle. He often readeth the lives of the primitive monks, hermits, and virgins, and wondreth not so much at their patient suffering and cheerful dying under persecuting emperors (though that indeed be very admirable) as at their daily temperance, abstinence, watchings, and constant prayers and mortifications in the times of peace and prosperity. To put on the profound humility, and the exact temperature of our Lord Jesus, with other exemplary virtues of that sort, and to keep them on in the sunshine and noon of prosperity, he findeth to be as necessary, and as difficult at least, as to be clothed with perfect patience and Christian fortitude in the cold midnight storms of persecution and adversity. He keepeth his watch and ward night and day against the proper and peculiar temptations of his state of life, which are principally these two, spiritual pride and impurity of heart: against these ghostly enemies he girdeth up his loins, keeps the imagination from roving, puts on the whole armour of God, and, by the virtue of the shield of faith, he is not afraid of the pestilence that walketh in darkness* [carnal impurity], *nor of the sickness that destroyeth at noonday* [ghostly pride and self-conceit.] *Other temptations he hath, which, like mortal enemies, may sometimes disquiet him likewise; for the human soul being bounded and kept in, in her sensitive faculty, will run out more or less in her intellectual. Original concupiscence is such an active thing, by reason of continual inward or outward temptations, that it is ever attempting or doing one mischief or other. Ambition, or untimely desire of promotion to a higher state or place, under colour of accommodation or necessary provision, is a common temptation to men of any eminency, especially being single men. Curiosity in prying into high speculative and unprofitable questions is another great stumbling-block to the holiness of scholars. These and many other spiritual wickednesses in high places doth the parson fear, or experiment,*[1] *or both, and that much more being single than if he were married; for then commonly the stream of temptations is turned another way, – into covetousness, love of pleasure, or ease, or the like. If the parson be unmarried, and means to continue so, he doth at least as much as hath been said.* If he be married, the choice of his wife was made rather by his ear than by his eye; his judgment, not his affection found out a fit wife for him, whose humble and liberal disposition he preferred before beauty, riches or honour. *He knew that (the good instrument of God to bring women to heaven) a wise and loving husband could, out of humility, produce any special grace of faith, patience, meekness, love, obedience, &c., and out of liberality make her fruitful in all good works.* As he is just in all things, so is he to his wife also, counting nothing so much his own as that he may be unjust unto it. Therefore he gives her respect both afore her servants and others, and half at least of the government of

---

1 That is, 'experience'.

the house, reserving so much of the affairs as serve for a diversion for him; yet never so giving over the reins but that he sometimes looks how things go, demanding an account, but not by the way of an account. And this must be done the oftener or the seldomer, according as he is satisfied of his wife's discretion.

3

The Priesthood

Blest Order, which in power dost so excel,
That with th' one hand thou liftest to the sky,
And with the other throwest down to hell
In thy just censures; fain would I draw nigh,
Fain put thee on, exchanging my lay-sword
   For that of th' holy word.

But thou art fire, sacred and hallow'd fire;
And I but earth and clay: should I presume
To wear thy habit, the severe attire
My slender compositions might consume.
I am both foul and brittle; much unfit
   To deal in holy Writ.

Yet have I often seen, by cunning hand
And force of fire, what curious things are made
Of wretched earth. Where once I scorn'd to stand,
That earth is fitted by the fire and trade
Of skilful artists, for the boards of those
   Who make the bravest shows.

But since those great ones, be they ne're so great,
Come from the earth, from whence those vessels come;
So that at once both feeder, dish, and meat
Have one beginning and one final sum:
I do not greatly wonder at the sight,
   If earth in earth delight.

But th' holy men of God such vessels are,
As serve him up, who all the world commands:

When God vouchsafeth to become our fare,
Their hands convey him, who conveys their hands.
O what pure things, most pure must those things be,
  Who bring my God to me!

Wherefore I dare not, I, put forth my hand
To hold the Ark, although it seems to shake
Through th' old sins and new doctrines of our land.
Only, since God doth often vessels make
Of lowly matter for high uses meet,
  I throw me at his feet.

There will I lie, until my Maker seek
For some mean stuff whereon to show his skill:
Then is my time. The distance of the meek
Doth flatter power. Lest good come short of ill
In praising might, the poor do by submission
  What pride by opposition.

4

Aaron

   Holiness on the head,
    Light and perfections on the breast,
Harmonious bells below, raising the dead
    To lead them unto life and rest.
     Thus are true Aarons drest.

   Profaneness in my head,
    Defects and darkness in my breast,
A noise of passions ringing me for dead
    Unto a place where is no rest,
     Poor priest thus am I drest.

   Only another head
    I have, another heart and breast,
Another music, making live not dead,
    Without whom I could have no rest:
     In him I am well drest.

Christ is my only head,
My alone only heart and breast,
My only music, striking me ev'n dead;
That to the old man I may rest,
And be in him new drest.

So holy in my head,
Perfect and light in my dear breast,
My doctrine tun'd by Christ (who is not dead,
But lives in me while I do rest)
Come people; Aaron's drest.

6

Prayer: The Soul in Paraphrase

For George Herbert, the nature of God is ultimately beyond the power of human words to express. Words may serve to describe and to praise but if we rely on them too much, as noted in the poem 'Jordan (2)', they merely shut us off from the ultimate source of light and life. For this reason, Herbert may have placed a high value on preaching but he had a still higher estimation of prayer. Even in *The Country Parson*, where there is a fairly didactic model of ministry, 'the Country Parson preacheth constantly' but not primarily in a catechetical way. He is to choose 'texts of devotion, not controversy, moving and ravishing texts, whereof the Scriptures are full' (Chapter VII). In the central section on public and personal prayer, in the long poem of moral and proverbial sayings, 'Perirrhanterium', the ultimate purpose of preaching is to lead people to prayer for 'Praying's the end of preaching' ('Perirrhanterium', line 410). And if prayer for Herbert is above all 'the Church's banquet', the prayer of the Church, the daily Offices and the Eucharist, there is beyond those structures and set formulae a promise of something ultimately intangible; a way of knowing that is perhaps mystical. As will be described later in this section, this is expressed beautifully yet allusively in the accumulated images of 'Prayer (1)'.

Prayer – General
Readings

1 Jordan (1)

2 Perirrhanterium, lines 385–455

1

Jordan (1)

Who says that fictions only and false hair
Become a verse? Is there in truth no beauty?
Is all good structure in a winding stair?
May no lines pass, except they do their duty
    Not to a true, but painted chair?

Is it no verse, except enchanted groves
And sudden arbours shadow coarse-spun lines?
Must purling streams refresh a lover's loves?
Must all be veil'd, while he that reads, divines,
    Catching the sense at two removes?

Shepherds are honest people; let them sing:
Riddle who list, for me, and pull for Prime:
I envy no man's nightingale or spring;
Nor let them punish me with loss of rhyme,
    Who plainly say, *My God, My King.*

2

Perirrhanterium

Restore to God his due in tithe and time:
A tithe purloin'd cankers the whole estate.
Sundays observe: think when the bells do chime,
'Tis angels' music; therefore come not late.
   God then deals blessings: If a king did so,
   Who would not haste, nay give, to see the show?

Twice on the day his due is understood;
For all the week thy food so oft he gave thee.
Thy cheer is mended; bate not of the food,
Because 'tis better, and perhaps may save thee.
   Thwart not th' Almighty God: O be not cross.
   Fast when thou wilt but then: 'tis gain, not loss.

Though private prayer be a brave design,
Yet public hath more promises, more love:
And love's a weight to hearts, to eyes a sign.
We all are but cold suitors; let us move
    Where it is warmest. Leave thy six and seven;
    Pray with the most: for where most pray, is heaven.

When once thy foot enters the church, be bare.
God is more there, than thou: for thou art there
Only by his permission. Then beware,
And make thy self all reverence and fear.
    Kneeling ne're spoil'd silk stocking: quit thy state.
    All equal are within the church's gate.

Resort to sermons, but to prayers most:
Praying's the end of preaching. O be drest;
Stay not for th' other pin: why thou hast lost
A joy for it worth worlds. Thus hell doth jest
    Away thy blessings, and extremely flout thee,
    Thy clothes being fast, but thy soul loose about thee.

In time of service seal up both thine eyes,
And send them to thine heart, that spying sin,
They may weep out the stains by them did rise:
Those doors being shut, all by the ear comes in.
    Who marks in church-time others' symmetry,
    Makes all their beauty his deformity.

Let vain or busy thoughts have there no part:
Bring not thy plough, thy plots, thy pleasures thither.
Christ purg'd his temple; so must thou thy heart.
All worldly thoughts are but thieves met together
    To cozen thee. Look to thy actions well:
    For churches are either our heav'n or hell.

Judge not the preacher; for he is thy Judge:
If thou mislike him, thou conceiv'st him not.
God calleth preaching folly. Do not grudge
To pick out treasures from an earthen pot.
    The worst speak something good: if all want sense,
    God takes a text, and preacheth patience.

He that gets patience, and the blessing which
Preachers conclude with, hath not lost his pains.
He that by being at church escapes the ditch,
Which he might fall in by companions, gains.
   He that loves God's abode, and to combine
   With saints on earth, shall one day with them shine.

Jest not at preachers' language, or expression:
How know'st thou, but thy sins made him miscarry?
Then turn thy faults and his into confession:
God sent him, whatsoe're he be: O tarry,
   And love him for his Master: his condition,
   Though it be ill makes him no ill Physician.

None shall in hell such bitter pangs endure,
As those who mock at God's way of salvation.
Whom oil and balsams kill, what salve can cure?
They drink with greediness a full damnation.
   The Jews refused thunder; and we, folly.
   Though God do hedge us in, yet who is holy?

Sum up at night, what thou hast done by day;
And in the morning, what thou hast to do.
Dress and undress thy soul: mark the decay
And growth of it: if with thy watch, that too
   Be down, then wind up both; since we shall be
   Most surely judg'd, make thy accounts agree.

Eucharist

The Eucharist is at the heart of Herbert's spiritual sensibilities and consequently features regularly throughout his poetry, at least implicitly. The poem on 'The Holy Communion' within the collection *The Temple* is far less explicitly theological, at least in the sense of apologetics, than another poem of the same name present in the manuscript known as 'W' yet omitted from the published collection. Herbert settles not simply theologically but spiritually for the mysterious, or mystical nature of the Eucharist whose powerful reality is beyond the powers of human definition.

Although Herbert does not become deeply embroiled in polemical argument about the Eucharist, it is possible to gain a feel for what Herbert believes. Throughout the poems he regularly uses words associated with the presence of Christ, the heavenly realm, the intersection of time and eternity, the banquet of the kingdom and the Eucharist as the medium for God's mystical union with us. The central section of poems, 'The Church', is immediately preceded by the final poem of 'The Church Porch', entitled 'Superliminary', where we are enjoined to 'approach, and taste/ The church's mystical repast'. This leads into the very first poem of the main section, 'The Altar', where, among other theological references, the eucharistic allusions could not be clearer. This in turn is followed by 'The Sacrifice' with its strong Protestant emphasis on Christ's saving passion yet resonances of the pre-Reformation liturgy of Holy Week. As an orthodox Protestant, Herbert's theology of the Eucharist embraced both a sense of Christ's presence to the communicants and also an emphasis that through reception Christians are brought to share in all the benefits of Christ's passion. The central section concludes with 'Love (3)' (quoted in the previous section) which suggests the earthly celebration of the Eucharist, the heavenly banquet beyond time and the connections between the two. Many of the phrases of the poem appear to echo the Exhortations attached to the service of Holy Communion in the *Book of Common Prayer*. Interestingly too, the final words, 'You must sit down, says Love, and taste my meat:/ So I did sit and eat' are followed immediately by the opening words of the *Gloria in Excelsis Deo* which act as a Post-Communion prayer in Cranmer's Prayer Book.

Eucharist
Readings

1 The Holy Communion (*The Temple*)

2 The Holy Communion (manuscript W)

1

The Holy Communion

Not in rich furniture, or fine array,
    Nor in a wedge of gold,
    Thou, who from me wast sold,
  To me dost now thy self convey;
For so thou should'st without me still have been,
    Leaving within me sin:

But by the way of nourishment and strength
    Thou creep'st into my breast;
    Making thy way my rest,
  And thy small quantities my length;
Which spread their forces into every part,
    Meeting sin's force and art.

Yet can these not get over to my soul,
    Leaping the wall that parts
    Our souls and fleshly hearts;
  But as th' outworks, they may control
My rebel-flesh, and carrying thy name,
    Affright both sin and shame.

Only thy grace, which with these elements comes,
    Knoweth the ready way,
    And hath the privy key,
  Op'ning the soul's most subtle rooms;
While those to spirits refin'd, at door attend
    Dispatches from their friend.

Give me my captive soul, or take
　My body also thither.
Another lift like this will make
　Them both to be together.

Before that sin turn'd flesh to stone,
　And all our lump to leaven,
A fervent sigh might well have blown
　Our innocent earth to heaven.

For sure when Adam did not know
　To sin, or sin to smother;
He might to heav'n from Paradise go,
　As from one room t'another.

Thou hast restor'd to us this ease
　By this thy heav'nly blood;
Which I can go to, when I please,
　And leave th' earth to their food.

2

The Holy Communion – from manuscript W

O gracious Lord, how shall I know
Whether in these gifts thou be so
　As thou art everywhere;
Or rather so, as thou alone
Tak'st all the Lodging, leaving none
　For thy poor creature there?

First I am sure, whether bread stay
Or whether Bread do fly away
　Concerneth bread, not me.
But that both thou and all thy train
Be there, to my truth, and my gain,
　Concerneth me and Thee.

And if in coming to thy foes
Thou dost come first to them, that shows
    The haste of thy good will.
Of if that thou two stations makest
In Bread and me, the way thou takest
    Is more, but for me still.

Then of this also I am sure
That thou didst all those pains endure
    To' abolish Sin, not Wheat.
Creatures are good, and have their place;
Sin only, which did all deface,
    Thou drivest from his seat.

I could believe an Impanation
At the rate of an Incarnation,
    If thou hadst died for Bread.
But that which made my soul to die,
My flesh, and fleshly villainy,
    That also made thee dead.

That flesh is there, mine eyes deny:
And what should flesh but flesh descry,
    The noblest sense of five?
If glorious bodies pass the sight,
Shall they be food and strength and might
    Even there, where they deceive?

Into my soul this cannot pass;
Flesh (though exalted) keeps his grass
    And cannot turn to soul.
Bodies and Minds are different Spheres,
Nor can they change their bounds and meres,
    But keep a constant Pole.

This gift of all gifts is the best,
Thy flesh the least that I request.
    Thou took'st that pledge from me:
Give me not that I had before,
Or give me that, so I have more;
    My God, give me all Thee.

Ways of Prayer

Contemporary spiritual seekers are often concerned to learn about particular techniques of prayer or meditation. To a large extent they would be disappointed by Herbert's writings. His *The Country Parson* makes some reference to private prayer (for example, Chapter X and Chapter XXXI) but there is little explicit teaching on ways of praying. Most of what can be drawn from Herbert is present only implicitly.

An important element of Herbert's teaching on prayer is his insistence on the importance of a daily pattern and on its connection with everyday life. Members of the parson's household are recommended to pray when they rise in the morning and before they go to sleep. The parson should also teach his parishioners that prayer twice a day, every day (and more on Sundays) is 'necessary' for all Christians. In the context of the priest's own prayers, Chapter VIII suggests that the morning prayers should request God to bless the work of the day and evening prayer should request God to accept the work of the day and to pardon any faults. In many respects, the poems 'Mattins' and 'Even-song' have much the same focus about prayer at either end of the day. As we have already seen, a form of examination of conscience is also recommended in 'Perirrhanterium'. A prayerful confession of faults is also hinted at in the poem 'The Method'. There are also references to praying at all times (perhaps including ejaculatory prayer) in *The Country Parson*, Chapter XXXV. The value of petitionary prayer is mentioned in several places and there are particular allusions to it in the poem, 'Prayer (2)'. Finally, *The Country Parson*, Chapter VI, explicitly titled 'The Parson Praying', suggests that people may be taught to make their own personal meditations in the pauses during the recitation of the public Offices.

Interestingly, in *The Country Parson*, Chapter XXXI, Herbert seems to recommend a more monastic pattern of daily prayer for those people he calls 'the godly'. This more intense pattern would add 'some hours of prayer, as at nine, or at three, or at midnight, or as they think fit'. Herbert refers to the long-standing tradition of these 'additionary' prayers which seems to imply knowledge of pre-Reformation monastic or collegiate patterns. However, it may also be that Herbert was thinking of his contemporary Nicholas Ferrar and the pattern at the Little Gidding community where a form of family quasi-monasticism was practised.

The poems of *The Temple* are themselves predominantly devotional. Indeed many of them are conversations of great intensity between Herbert and God. As his poem 'The Quiddity' makes clear, Herbert understood poetry itself to be a form of prayer. 'My God, a verse is not a crown/ ... But it is that which while I use/ I am with thee, and *Most take all*.' The conversational poems of 'The Church' parallel similar styles of intimate prayer that spiritual teachers of the Catholic Reformation recommended and describe as 'Colloquies'. Many of Herbert's poems are meditations with biblical references and from Chapter IV in *The Country Parson* it is clear that Herbert was familiar with the concept of biblical meditation, although no method is indicated.

The question arises whether Herbert shows an awareness of contemplative forms of prayer. There is certainly no explicit teaching. However a strong sense of contemplative awareness and experience shines through a number of poems – a kind of awareness that inspired the English composer Ralph Vaughan Williams to call his orchestral and choral cycle of five of Herbert's poems *Mystical Songs*. The second part of the poem 'The Holy Communion' (sometimes printed as a separate poem) suggests that prayer has the capacity to transport us from this time and space to heaven and to the kind of relationship with God that Adam once knew before the Fall. In one of the poems set to music by Vaughan Williams, 'Easter' (sometimes divided into 1 and 2), there are hints of the writer being transported to another level of awareness where all time is caught up into the eternal present of Christ's Easter triumph. In another of the *Five Mystical Songs*, 'The Call', an intensity of experience is expressed that certainly moves beyond the conventional. Finally, of course, an intense spiritual intimacy and presence is evident in the poem 'Love (3)' already quoted and which provoked some kind of mystical experience in Simone Weil.

Ways of Prayer
Readings

1 *The Country Parson*, Chapter XXXI

2 Prayer (2)

3 The Call

I

The Country Parson, Chapter XXXI
The Parson in Liberty

The Country Parson observing the manifold wiles of Satan (who plays his part sometimes in drawing God's servants from him, sometimes in perplexing them in the service of God) stands fast in the liberty wherewith Christ hath made us free. This liberty he compasseth by one distinction, and that is, of what is necessary and what is additionary. As for example: it is necessary that all Christians should pray twice a day every day of the week, and four times on Sunday if they be well. This is so necessary and essential to a Christian that he cannot without this maintain himself in a Christian state. Besides this, the godly have ever added some hours of prayer, as at nine, or at three, or at midnight, or as they think fit and see cause, or rather as God's spirit leads them. But these prayers are not necessary, but additionary. Now it so happens that the godly petitioner upon some emergent interruption in the day, or by oversleeping himself at night, omits his additionary prayer. Upon this his mind begins to be perplexed and troubled, and Satan, who knows the exigent, blows the fire, endeavouring to disorder the Christian, and put him out of his station, and to enlarge the perplexity until it spread and taint his other duties or piety, which none can perform so well in trouble as in calmness. Here the parson interposeth with his distinction, and shows the perplexed Christian that his prayer being additionary, not necessary – taken in, not commanded – the omission thereof upon just occasion ought by no means to trouble him. God knows the occasion as well as he, and he is as a gracious Father, who more accepts a common course of devotion than dislikes an occasional interruption. And of this he is so to assure himself as to admit no scruple, but to go on as cheerfully as if he had not been interrupted. By this it is evident that the distinction is of singular use and comfort, especially to pious minds, which are ever tender and delicate. But here there are two cautions to be added. First, that this interruption proceed not out of slackness or coldness, which will appear if the pious soul foresee and prevent such interruptions, what he may, before they come, and when for all that they do come, he be a little affected therewith, but not afflicted or troubled; if he resent it to a mislike, but not a grief. Secondly, that this interruption proceed not out of shame. As for example: a godly man, not out of superstition, but of reverence to God's house, resolves

whenever he enters into a church to kneel down and pray, either blessing God that he will be pleased to dwell among men, or beseeching
him that whenever he repairs to his house he may behave himself so as
befits so great a presence, and this briefly. But it happens that near the
place where he is to pray he spies some scoffing ruffian, who is likely
to deride him for his pains: if he now shall, either for fear or shame,
break his custom, he shall do passing ill: so much the rather ought he
to proceed, as that by this he may take into his prayer humiliation also.
On the other side, if I am to visit the sick in haste, and my nearest way
lie through the church, I will not doubt to go without staying to pray
there (but only, as I pass, in my heart), because this kind of prayer is
additionary, not necessary, and the other duty overweighs it, so that if
any scruple arise I will throw it away, and be most confident that God
is not displeased. This distinction may run through all Christian duties,
and it is a great stay and settling to religious souls.

2

Prayer (2)

Of what an easy quick access,
My blessed Lord, art thou! how suddenly
    May our requests thine ear invade!
To show that state dislikes not easiness.
If I but lift mine eyes, my suit is made:
Thou canst no more not hear, than thou canst die.

Of what supreme almighty power
Is thy great arm which spans the east and west,
    And tacks the centre to the sphere!
By it do all things live their measur'd hour:
We cannot ask the thing, which is not there,
Blaming the shallowness of our request.

Of what unmeasurable love
Art thou possest, who, when thou couldst not die,
    Wert fain to take our flesh and curse,
And for our sakes in person sin reprove,
That by destroying that which ty'd thy purse,
Thou mightst make way for liberality!

Since then these three wait on thy throne,
Ease, *Power*, and *Love*; I value prayer so,
   That were I to leave all but one,
Wealth, fame, endowments, virtues, all should go;
I and dear prayer would together dwell,
And quickly gain, for each inch lost, an ell.

3

The Call

Come, my Way, my Truth, my Life:
Such a Way, as gives us breath:
Such a Truth, as ends all strife:
And such a Life, as killeth death.

Come, my Light, my Feast, my Strength:
Such a Light, as shows a feast:
Such a Feast, as mends in length:
Such a Strength, as makes his guest.

Come, my Joy, my Love, my Heart:
Such a Joy, as none can move:
Such a Love, as none can part:
Such a Heart, as joys in love.

The poem 'Prayer (1)'

Arguably the most striking lines of George Herbert concerning prayer occur in the first poem of that name in *The Temple*. This is an extra-ordinary poem even in its technical construction. It is a sonnet that has no main verb but simply a succession of brief metaphorical phrases tumbling one after another. The lines rely on a cumulative effect rather than on a conclusive definition. In attempting to express the nature of prayer, Herbert turns away from the obvious path of simile: 'prayer is like …' Metaphor provides greater imaginative scope that enables him to draw the reader beyond the limits of what is expressible. Paradoxic-ally, therefore, Herbert offers many images of prayer and yet also sug-gests an underlying truth that prayer cannot ultimately be described. It is a mysterious process that enables people to touch ultimate Mystery. Herbert's range of metaphors swings between time and eternity, the everyday and heaven, in just the same way that prayer forms a bridge between two worlds.

The poem begins with the phrase 'the Church's banquet'. As we might expect in Herbert, all prayer is to be understood as common prayer, the prayer of the Church. The metaphor has another dimen-sion as well. A banquet is a meal. Prayer is spiritual food – a metaphor deepened by the use of others later in the poem, 'exalted Manna' and 'land of spices'. The term 'heavenly banquet' was Richard Hooker's preferred eucharistic metaphor and Herbert's own poem 'The Banquet' and his banquet imagery elsewhere in the collection are arguably eucharistic.

Prayer is also deeply personal. It is 'the soul's blood', the source of life coursing through the veins. It is also 'the soul in paraphrase': it expands the soul to its full potential and is the most perfect expression of the deepest self. 'God's breath in man returning to his birth' suggests that prayer has the capacity to return people to the first moment of creation, the source of life created by God.

The richness of the imagery and its sensuous quality may give the impression that prayer is merely 'softness, and peace, and joy, and love, and bliss'. However, hints of spiritual struggle save the poem from feel-ing out of touch with the complexity and, at times, confusion of human experience. 'Engine against th' Almighty' speaks of prayer as laying siege to God. This is an ambiguous image that suggests both persever-ance and combat. Herbert is not afraid to admit that he has frequently battled with God. In the poem 'Artillery' he says to God, 'Then we are shooters both, and Thou dost deign/ To enter combat with us, and contest/ With thine own clay.' In this sense of struggle with God, Herbert echoes the emotional tone of his favourite Book of Psalms.

'Heart in pilgrimage'. In his commitment to prayer, George Herbert came to understand that the depths of a person could be radically changed. Underlying his spiritual journey was an experience of transformation whereby fear of God's wrath gave way to a realization of God's loving acceptance in Christ. The graphic metaphor, 'Christ-side-piercing spear' reflects similar imagery in another poem, 'The Bag'. The wound in Christ's side becomes a space where believers may safely deposit their messages to God.

Yet, in the midst of his inner struggle, Herbert seems to have had a profound sense that the world of everyday experience was filled with the presence of God. Through its powerful and cumulative use of images, the poem offers an extraordinarily rich vision of the sacred as something to be encountered within the ordinary and yet which carries people beyond the ordinary. Natural and biblical allusions combine with strikingly original images ('Church-bells beyond the stars heard') to suggest that the mundane is transfigured by the radiance of divine glory. 'Heaven in ordinary'. Interestingly, an 'ordinary' in Herbert's day could also mean the regular menu of cheap food served in wayside inns and the rough part of the inn where the common menu was served. Perhaps there are echoes here of the poem 'Redemption' where God is found among the 'ragged noise and mirth' made by precisely the kinds of disreputable people one might find in an 'ordinary'. 'The six-days-world transposing in an hour'. Herbert's love of musical imagery appears on many occasions throughout his poetry. The next line speaks of prayer as 'a kind of tune'. Prayer *transposes* the six-days quotidian world into another key.

For George Herbert, in prayer humans come as close to God as is possible in mundane existence. The poem concludes with that pregnant but elusive phrase, 'something understood'. In the end, all attempts to describe prayer fail. The final metaphor is a paradoxical climax to the poem because it leaves the reader without a definitive conclusion. It is deliberately open-ended. 'Understood' is not objective knowledge but something tentative and incomplete. In that 'something' is the hint that on the margins of human awareness lies the hope and promise of a final resolution, the ultimate seeing and hearing that Herbert's poem celebrates.

'Prayer (1)'
Reading

1 Prayer (1)

I

Prayer (1)

Prayer the Church's banquet, Angels' age,
   God's breath in man returning to his birth,
   The soul in paraphrase, heart in pilgrimage,
The Christian plummet sounding heav'n and earth;
Engine against th' Almighty, sinners' tower,
   Reversed thunder, Christ-side-piercing spear,
   The six-days-world transposing in an hour,
A kind of tune, which all things hear and fear;
Softness, and peace, and joy, and love, and bliss,
   Exalted Manna, gladness of the best,
   Heaven in ordinary, man well drest,
The milky way, the bird of Paradise,
   Church-bells beyond the stars heard, the soul's blood,
   The land of spices; something understood.

7

Pastoral Care and Service

George Herbert's essentially pastoral purpose is implicit throughout his writings, even in the way that the poetic collection *The Temple* is structured, and is also explicit in some individual poems. However, Herbert gives greatest attention to a spirituality of service in the prose treatise, *The Country Parson*. It is impossible to ignore the fact that, in the religious and social context of his times, Herbert inevitably views pastoral service as predominantly the role of the ordained priest. However, Herbert also hints that a spirituality of service is part of the wider Christian vocation when he suggests a role for members of the priest's family and household in visiting the sick, in the healing ministry and above all in spiritual conversation.

In Herbert's own terms, care is not simply about specific actions but something that involves the whole person of the priest or Christian. The sorrows, joys, grief and glories of the parish become those of the country parson. To serve is to act as an agent of reconciliation, to visit the sick and to exhort others to a life of grace. To be holy is to share oneself with others. George Herbert was convinced that the one thing that mattered for a Christian was to worship God in spirit and truth, living always in a spirit of repentance. However, the process of living this out inevitably overflows into a service of others.

To be pastoral is to be God's 'watchman' (*The Country Parson*, Chapter XVIII), to be in God's place and to help to discharge God's promises (Chapter XX). More particularly, a spirituality of service or pastoral care is Christ-centred. The pastor is the deputy of Christ (Chapter I) to continue his work of reconciliation. It is necessary, though difficult, for the pastor 'to put on the profound humility, and the exact temperature of our Lord Jesus' (Chapter IX).

The Ecclesial Context

We have already seen that the spirituality of the seventeenth-century Church of England is overtly focused on the life of the Church. Herbert's approach to preaching and teaching is always within an ecclesial context. For him, the Church serves because God serves and because the Church serves the pastor serves. If the parson is 'the deputy of Christ', the minister is also and always the representative of the Church as Herbert indicates in his comments on the importance of using the official Catechism (Chapters V & XXI) or of obeying the bishop (Chapter XIX). Equally, just as preaching should lead to prayer, so one important dimension of Herbert's overall teaching is preparation for the liturgy and the sacraments of the Church, especially the Eucharist (Chapter XXII).

Herbert shared with his mentor Bishop Lancelot Andrewes and with the controversial and reforming Archbishop Laud the aim of renewing the whole of society through the agency of the Church. The teaching and sacraments of the Church gather people together as agents of renewal and commitment as much in the nation as in the Church itself. Thus, Herbert's approach to service is not simply directed towards the individual person in isolation. All service in the model of Christ is to build up the community. Herbert has a very social and collective understanding of human nature.

Service – Ecclesial
Reading

1 *The Country Parson*, Chapter XIX

I

The Country Parson, Chapter XIX
The Parson in Reference

The Country Parson is sincere and upright in all his relations. And first, he is just to his country; as when he is set at an armour or horse, he borrows them not to serve the turn, nor provides slight and unuseful, but such as are every way fitting to do his country true and laudable service when occasion requires. To do otherwise is deceit, and therefore not for him, who is hearty and true in all his ways, as being the servant of him in whom there was no guile. Likewise in any other country duty, he considers what is the end of any command, and then he suits things faithfully according to that end. Secondly, he carries himself very respectively, as to all the fathers of the Church, so especially to his diocesan, honouring him both in word and behaviour, and resorting unto him in any difficulty either in his studies or in his parish. He observes visitations, and being there, makes due use of them, as of clergy councils, for the benefit of the diocese. And therefore, before he comes, having observed some defects in the ministry, he then, either in sermon, if he preach, or at some other time of the day, propounds among his brethren what were fitting to be done. Thirdly, he keeps good correspondence with all the neighbouring pastors round about him, performing for them any ministerial office, which is not to the prejudice of his own parish. Likewise he welcomes to his house any minister, how poor or mean soever, with as joyful a countenance as if he were to entertain some great lord. Fourthly, he fulfils the duty and debt of neighbourhood to all the parishes which are near him; for the Apostle's rule, *Philip.* 4 being admirable and large, that *we should do whatsoever things are honest, or just, or pure, or lovely, or of good report, if there be any virtue or any praise.* And neighbourhood being ever reputed, even among the heathen, as an obligation to do good, rather than to those that are farther, where things are otherwise equal, therefore he satisfies this duty also. Especially if God have sent any calamity, either by fire or famine, to any neighbouring parish, then he expects no brief; but taking his parish together *the next Sunday*, or *holy day*, and exposing to them the uncertainty of human affairs, none knowing whose turn may be next; and then, when he hath affrighted them with this, exposing the obligation of charity and neighbourhood, he first gives himself liberally, and then incites them to give – making together a sum either to be sent, or, which were more comfortable, all together choosing some fit day to carry it themselves, and cheer the afflicted. So, if any neighbouring village be overburdened with poor, and his own less charged, he finds some way of relieving it, and reducing the manna and bread of charity to some equality, representing to his people that the blessing of God to them ought to make them the more charitable, and not the less, lest he cast their neighbours' poverty on them also.

Charity

At the heart of Herbert's spirituality of service lies the classic Christian virtue of charity, or love. 'The Country Parson is full of charity; it is his predominant element' (Chapter XII). Insofar as charity involves giving material assistance to those in need, the priest, and by extension every Christian, is to do this from personal possessions so that charity actually costs something. Indeed, the priest should take every opportunity of 'exposing the obligation of charity' to his parishioners, particularly when he invites them to see the neediness of people beyond the boundaries of their own village (Chapter XIX).

Herbert's historically conditioned notion that charity should aim to make people dependent is highly questionable. However, there is more to be commended in his belief in the importance of courtesy. In one sense, material charity to the poor is another form of what Herbert calls a 'debt' of courtesy. In some cases, courtesy is expressed in hospitality and Herbert is quite clear that the priest should not hesitate to have the poor to dinner and to serve them personally. However, it may be that such hospitality is not what they need most. True courtesy may mean that we have to let needy people decide for themselves what they most need rather than impose our desires upon them. Thus, the money that might be used to offer poor people good food might be better employed if it were given to the poor themselves to be used by them 'to their own advantage, and suitably to their needs' (Chapter XI).

Charity
Readings

1 *The Country Parson*, Chapter XI
2 *The Country Parson*, Chapter XII

I

The Country Parson, Chapter XI
The Parson's Courtesy

The Country Parson owing a debt of charity to the poor and of courtesy to his other parishioners, he so distinguisheth, that he keeps his money for the poor, and his table for those that are above alms. Not but that the poor are welcome also to his table, whom he sometimes purposely takes home with him, setting them close by him, and carving for them, both for his own humility and their comfort, who are much cheered with such friendliness. But since both is to be done, the better sort invited, and meaner relieved, he chooseth rather to give the poor money, which they can better employ to their own advantage, and suitably to their needs, than so much given in meat at dinner. Having then invited some of his parish, he taketh his times to do the like to the rest; so that in the compass of the year he hath them all with him, because country people are very observant of such things, and will not be persuaded but, being not invited, they are hated. Which persuasion the parson by all means avoids, knowing that where there are such conceits there is no room for his doctrine to enter. Yet doth he oftenest invite those whom he sees take the best courses, that so both they may be encouraged to persevere, and others spurred to do well, that they may enjoy the like courtesy. For though he desire that all should live well and virtuously, not for any reward of his, but for virtue's sake; yet that will not be so; and therefore as God, although we should love him only for his own sake, yet out of his infinite pity hath set forth heaven for a reward to draw men to piety, and is content if at least so they will become good: so the country parson, who is a diligent observer and tracker of God's ways, sets up as many encouragements to goodness as he can, both in honour, and profit, and fame, that he may, if not the best way, yet any way, make his parish good.

2

The Country Parson, Chapter XII
The Parson's Charity

The Country Parson is full of charity; it is his predominant element. For many and wonderful things are spoken of thee, thou great virtue. To charity is given the covering of sins, *I Peter* 4: 8; and the forgiveness of sins, *Matthew* 6: 14, *Luke* 7: 47; the fulfilling of the law, *Romans* 13: 10; the life of faith, *James* 2: 26; the blessings of this life, *Proverbs* 22: 9, *Psalm* 41: 2; and the reward of the next, *Matthew* 25: 35. In brief, it is the body of religion (*John* 13: 35), and the top of Christian virtues (*I Corinthians* 13). Wherefore all his works relish of charity. When he riseth in the morning he bethinketh himself what good deeds he can do that day, and presently doth them; counting that day lost wherein he hath not exercised his charity. He first considers his own parish, and takes care that there be not a beggar or idle person in his parish, but that all be in a competent way of getting their living. This he effects either by bounty, or by persuasion, or by authority, making use of that excellent statute which binds all parishes to maintain their own. If his parish be rich, he exacts this of them; if poor, and he able, he easeth them therein. But he gives no set pension to any; for this in time will lose the name and effect of charity with the poor people, though not with God; for then they will reckon upon it as on a debt; and if it be taken away, though justly, they will murmur and repine as much as he that is disseized of his own inheritance. But the parson having a double aim, and making a hook of his charity, causeth them still to depend on him; and so by continual and fresh bounties, unexpected to them, but resolved to himself, he wins them to praise God more, to live more religiously, and to take more pains in their vocation, as not knowing when they shall be relieved; which otherwise they would reckon upon and turn to idleness. Besides this general provision, he hath other times of opening his hand; as at great festivals and communions; not suffering any that day that he receives to want a good meal suiting to the joy of the occasion. But specially at hard times and dearths, he even parts his living and life among them, giving some corn outright, and selling other at under rates; and when his own stock serves not, working those that are able to the same charity, still pressing it in the pulpit and out of the pulpit, and never leaving them till he obtain his desire. Yet in all his charity he distinguisheth, giving them most who live best, and take most pains, and are most charged; so is his charity in effect a sermon. After the consideration of his own parish, he enlargeth himself, if he be able, to the neighbourhood, for that also is some kind of obligation; so doth he also to those at his door, whom God puts in his way and makes his neighbours. But these he helps not without some testimony, except the evidence of the misery bring testimony with it. For though these testimonies also may be falsified, yet considering that the law allows these in case they be true, but allows by no means to give without testimony, as he obeys authority in the one, so that being once satisfied he allows his charity some blindness in the other; especially, since of the two commands we are more enjoined to be charitable than wise. But evident miseries have a natural privilege and exemption from all law. Whenever he gives anything, and sees them labour in thanking of him, he exacts of them to let him alone, and say rather, God be praised, God be glorified; that so the thanks may go the right way, and thither only where they are only due. So doth he also before giving make them say their prayers first, or the Creed, and ten Commandments, and as he finds them perfect, rewards them the more. For other givings are lay and secular, but this is to give like a priest.

Spiritual Guidance

As well as teacher and leader of worship, the parson in Herbert's writings is a spiritual guide to individuals as well as to the whole community. Before all else he 'digested all the points of consolation' (Chapter XV). The priest seeks to alleviate scruples particularly when advising people about their life of prayer, not least the problem of distractions especially during additional prayer done out of generosity of spirit rather than duty (Chapter XXXI).

In general the priest is to attend to the spiritual state of his parishioners, responding to each according to their need. Herbert advises the parson to note the spiritual 'movements' within his parishioners and to react appropriately. So the priest is to advise vigilance to people who seem rather untroubled spiritually yet he is to fortify and strengthen those who are tempted (Chapter XXXIV).

Herbert is very much in the tradition of the Prayer Book as well as of the other Caroline Divines, such as Jeremy Taylor, when he recommends 'particular confession' as a comfort and remedy to those who are afflicted in any way, physically or spiritually (Chapter XV). Individual confession was to be less narrowly focused on the power of absolution than it was in the Roman Catholic tradition and more broadly focused on guidance. Thus in the 1562 (and 1662) *Book of Common Prayer*, those with unquiet consciences should seek not merely absolution but also 'ghostly counsel and advice'. Bishop Jeremy Taylor linked spiritual guidance to confession in his *Ductor Dubitantium*. So did Francis White in his 1625 *A Reply to the Jesuit Fisher*: 'The true ends of private confession are these which follow: First, to inform, instruct and counsel Christian people ... ' The 1634 Irish Canons suggest the same: 'Finding themselves either extreme dull or much troubled in mind, they do resort unto God's ministers to receive from them as well advice and counsel for the quickening of their dead hearts and the subduing of those corruptions whereunto they have been subject as the benefit of Absolution.'

Spiritual guidance as expressed by Herbert is something to be considered ordinary rather than extraordinary. There is a thread of what might be called spiritual conversation that runs throughout the whole of *The Country Parson*. This takes place not only in church or on religious occasions but while the priest is entertaining in his own house (Chapter VIII) or visiting people's homes and on the occasions of their everyday work (Chapter XIV). All the members of the priest's household are to share in this ministry of spiritual conversation (Chapter X).

Spiritual Guidance
Reading

1 *The Country Parson*, Chapter XV

I

The Country Parson, Chapter XV
The Parson Comforting

The Country Parson, when any of his cure is sick, or afflicted with loss of friend or estate, or any ways distressed, fails not to afford his best comforts, and rather goes to them than sends for the afflicted, though they can and otherwise ought to come to him. To this end he hath thoroughly digested all the points of consolation, as having continual use of them, such as are from God's general providence extended even to lilies; from his particular, to his church; from his promises; from the examples of all saints that ever were; from Christ himself, perfecting our redemption no other way than by sorrow; from the benefit of affliction which softens and works the stubborn heart of man; from the certainty both of deliverance and reward if we faint not; from the miserable comparison of the moment of griefs here with the weight of joys hereafter. *Besides this, in his visiting the sick or otherwise afflicted, he followeth the Church's counsel, namely, in persuading them to particular confession; labouring to make them understand the great good use of this ancient and pious ordinance, and how necessary it is in some cases; he also urgeth them to do some pious charitable works as a necessary evidence and fruit of their faith at that time especially: the participation of the Holy Sacrament, how comfortable and sovereign a medicine it is to all sin-sick souls; what strength, and joy, and peace it administers against all temptations, even to death itself he plainly and generally intimateth all this to the disaffected or sick person, that so the hunger and thirst after it may come rather from themselves than from his persuasion.*

The Service of Healing

Apart from spiritual comfort, Herbert shows a marked interest in physical healing. How this interest originated is uncertain. It may reflect what we know of Herbert's own history of poor health or it may have arisen from contact with country traditions of herbal remedies.

The Country Parson, Chapter XXIII offers the most extensive treatment of physical healing. This is to be one of the parson's crucial tasks in the parish. The parson is to make sure that basic medical care is provided. Preferably he or his wife is to be a physician. Indeed, earlier in Chapter X, skill in healing is one of the three basic qualities to be hoped for in a priest's wife. Even the priest's children are to have a modest healing role at least as visitors of the sick. Herbert lists other alternative approaches if the parson and his wife have no skill in medicine. The priest could keep a physician in his household if he can afford it or he could develop a friendly relationship with a nearby physician whom he can call into the parish when needed. Herbert shows similar concern to encourage self-help as he does in the context of charitable gifts to the poor. In Chapter XIV Herbert even suggests that the parson should pass on some medicinal knowledge to parishioners during his visits.

Herbert seeks to persuade the aspiring parish priest that herbal medicine is not a difficult skill to learn. He recommends certain books and also the development of a herb garden. A few examples of herbs and their uses are mentioned. Herbert argues that herbs are more natural and cheaper than drugs from an apothecary in the bigger towns. Certainly 'home-bred' herbs are to be preferred to spices and 'outlandish gums' which Herbert condemns as vanities.

Herbert is concerned to maintain the link between this concern for physical healing and spiritual ministry. Although the priest's herb garden is a 'shop' of cures to replace the city apothecary, it may also become an extension of the church building. 'In curing of any, the parson and his family use to premise prayers, for this is to cure like a parson, and this raiseth the action from the shop to the church.'

Healing

Reading

1 *The Country Parson*, Chapter XXIII

I

The Country Parson, Chapter XXIII
The Parson's Completeness

The Country Parson desires to be all to his parish, and not only a pastor, but a lawyer also, and a physician. Therefore he endures not that any of his flock should go to law; but in any controversy, that they should resort to him as their judge. To this end he hath gotten to himself some insight in things ordinarily incident and controverted, by experience and by reading some initiatory treatises in the law, with Dalton's 'Justice of Peace', and the abridgements of the statutes, as also by discourse with men of that profession, whom he hath ever some cases to ask when he meets with them – holding that rule that to put men to discourse of that wherein they are most eminent is the most gainful way of conversation. Yet, whenever any controversy is brought to him, he never decides it alone, but sends for three or four of the ablest of the parish to hear the cause with him, whom he makes to deliver their opinion first; out of which he gathers, in case he be ignorant himself, what to hold; and so the thing passeth with more authority and less envy. In judging, he follows that which is altogether right; so that if the poorest man of the parish detain but a pin unjustly from the richest, he absolutely restores it as a judge; but when he hath so done, then he assumes the parson, and exhorts to charity. Nevertheless, there may happen sometimes some cases wherein he chooseth to permit his parishioners rather to make use of the law than himself; as in cases of an obscure and dark nature not easily determinable by lawyers themselves; or in cases of high consequence, as establishing of inheritances; or, lastly, when the persons in difference are of a contentious disposition and cannot be gained, but that they still fall from all compromises that have been made. But then he shows them how to go to law, even as brethren, and not as enemies, neither avoiding therefore one another's company, much less defaming one another. Now, as the parson is in law, so is he in sickness also: if there be any of his flock sick, he is their physician, or at least his wife, of whom, instead of the qualities of the world, he asks no other but to have the skill of healing a wound or helping the sick. But if neither himself nor his wife have the skill, and his means serve, he keeps some young practitioner in his house for the benefit of his parish, whom yet he ever exhorts not to exceed his bounds, but in tickle cases to call in help. If all fail, then he keeps good correspondence with some neighbour physician, and entertains him for the cure of his parish. Yet it is easy for any scholar to attain to such a measure of physic, as may be of much use to him both for himself and others. This is done by seeing one anatomy, reading one book of physic, having one herbal by him. And let Fernelius be the physic author, for he writes briefly, neatly, and judiciously; especially let his method of physic be diligently perused, as being the practical part and of most use. Now, both the reading of him and the knowing of herbs may be done at such times as they may be an help and a recreation to more divine studies, Nature serving grace both in comfort of diversion and the benefit of application when need requires; as also by way of illustration, even as our Saviour made plants and seeds to teach the people; for he was the true householder, who bringeth out of his treasure things new and old – the old things of philosophy, and the new of grace – and maketh the one serve the other. And I conceive our Saviour did this for three reasons: First; that by familiar things he might make his doctrine slip the more easily into the hearts even of the meanest. Secondly, that labouring people (whom he chiefly considered) might have everywhere monuments of his doctrine, remembering in gardens, his mustard seed and lilies; in the field, his seed-corn and tares; and so not be drowned altogether in the works of their vocation, but sometimes lift up their minds to better things even in the midst of their pains. Thirdly, that he might set a copy for parsons. In the knowledge of simples, wherein the manifold wisdom of God is wonderfully to be seen, one thing would be carefully observed: which is, to know what herbs may be used instead of drugs of the same nature, and to make the garden the shop; for home-bred medicines are both more easy for the parson's purse, and more familiar for all men's bodies. So, where the apothecary useth either for loosing, rhubarb, or for binding, bolearmena, the parson useth damask or white roses for the one, and plantain, shepherd's-purse, knot-grass for the other, and that with better success. As for spices, he doth not only prefer home-bred things before them, but condemns them for vanities, and so shuts them out of his family, esteeming that there is no spice comparable for herbs to rosemary, time, savory, mints; and for seeds to Fennel, and caraway-seeds. Accordingly, for salves, his wife seeks not the city, but prefers her garden and fields, before all outlandish gums. And surely hyssop, valerian, mercury, adder's-tongue, yarrow, melilot, and St. John's wort made into a salve, and elder, camomile, mallows, comphrey, and smallage made into a poultice, have done great and rare cures. In curing of any the parson and his family use to premise prayers, for this is to cure like a parson, and this raiseth the action from the shop to the church. But though the parson sets forward all charitable deeds, yet he looks not in this point of curing beyond his own parish, except the person be so poor that he is not able to reward the physician; for as he is charitable, so he is just also. Now, it is a justice and debt to the commonwealth he lives in not to encroach on others' professions, but to live on his own. And justice is the ground of charity.

The Art of Complete and Adaptable Care

From his interest in healing, it is clear that Herbert's understanding of a spirituality of service is broadly based. It expresses a sense of the completeness and adaptability of pastoral care. First the parson should seek to be involved in every aspect of the life of the parish. To some contemporary readers this may sound oppressive at first glance. However, in other ways, such a vision suggests a thoroughly modern holistic model of pastoral care. 'The Country Parson desires to be all to his parish, and not only a pastor, but a lawyer also, and a physician' (Chapter XXIII). As well as being teacher, leader of worship and herbal doctor, the parson is to offer a modest form of legal advice. Clearly local knowledge is the bedrock of effective pastoral response and visiting is described as the most productive means (Chapter XIV).

In Herbert's mind, pastoral care must take a thorough account of individual personalities and of specific contexts. When the parson teaches he is to address concrete needs and to adopt means that speak directly to the condition of the people to whom he ministers. Country folk, for example, were deemed to be better suited to stories and sayings than to anything more abstract (e.g. Chapter VII). In a country context, the priest needs to take account not only of the nature of country people ('which are thick and heavy') but also of their work. The priest should place an emphasis on divine providence to counter a tendency by people to over-emphasize the natural order of things – in other words, fatalism (Chapter XXX). Herbert's parson respects ancient country customs, particularly those, such as processions or the blessing of lights, which have a devotional origin (Chapter XXXV). The priest should also be familiar with the everyday life of agriculture. 'He condescends even to the knowledge of tillage and pasturage, and makes great use of them in teaching, because people by what they understand are best led to what they understand not' (Chapter IV).

Complete Care
Reading

1 *The Country Parson*, Chapter XXXIV

I

The Country Parson, Chapter XXXIV
The Parson's Dexterity in Applying of Remedies

The Country Parson knows that there is a double state of a Christian even in this life: the one military, the other peaceable. The military is when we are assaulted with temptations, either from within or from without; the peaceable is when the devil for a time leaves us, as he did our Saviour, and the angels minister to us their own food, even joy, and peace, and comfort in the Holy Ghost. These two states were in our Saviour, not only in the beginning of his preaching, but afterwards also, as *Matt.* 22: 35: He was tempted, and *Luke* 10: 21: He rejoiced in spirit; and they must be likewise in all that are his. Now the parson having a spiritual judgment, according as he discovers any of his flock to be in one or the other state, so he applies himself to them. Those that he finds in the peaceable state, he adviseth to be very vigilant, and not to let go the reins as soon as the horse goes easy. Particularly he counselleth them to two things: First, to take heed lest their quiet betray them (as it is apt to do) to a coldness and carelessness in their devotions, but to labour still to be as fervent in Christian duties as they remember themselves were when affliction did blow the coals. Secondly, not to take the full compass and liberty of their peace: not to eat of all those dishes at table which even their present health otherwise admits; nor to store their house with all those furnitures which even their present plenty of wealth otherwise admits; nor when they are among them that are merry, to extend themselves to all that mirth which the present occasion of wit and company otherwise admits; but to put bounds and hoops to their joys; so will they last the longer, and, when they depart, return the sooner. If we would judge ourselves, we should not be judged; and if we would bound ourselves, we should not be bounded. But if they shall fear that at such or such a time their peace and mirth have carried them further than this moderation, then to take Job's admirable course, who sacrificed lest his children should have transgressed in their mirth; so let them go, and find some poor afflicted soul, and there be bountiful and liberal; for with such sacrifices God is well pleased. Those that the parson finds in the military state, he fortifies and strengthens with his utmost skill. Now, in those that are tempted, whatsoever is unruly falls upon two heads: either they think that there is none that can or will look after things, but all goes by chance or wit; or else, though there be a great Governor of all things, yet to them he is lost – as if they said, God doth forsake and persecute them, and there is none to deliver them. If the parson suspect the first, and find sparks of such thoughts now and then to break forth, then, without opposing directly (for disputation is no cure for atheism), he scatters in his discourse three sorts of arguments: the first taken from nature, the second from the law, the third from grace.

For nature, he sees not how a house could be either built without a builder, or kept in repair without a housekeeper. He conceives not possibly how the winds should blow so much as they can, and the sea rage so much as it can, and all things do what they can, and all, not only without dissolution of the whole, but also of any part, by taking away so much as the usual seasons of summer and winter, earing and harvest. Let the weather be what it will, still we have bread, though sometimes more, sometimes less; wherewith also a careful Joseph might meet. He conceives not possibly how he that would believe a divinity, if he had been at the Creation of all things, should less believe it, seeing the preservation of all things; for preservation is a creation, and more, it is a continued creation, and a creation every moment.

Secondly, for the law: there may be so evident though unused a proof of divinity taken from thence, that the atheist or epicurean can have nothing to contradict. The Jews yet live and are known: they have their law and language bearing witness to them, and they to it; they are circumcised to this day, and expect the promises of the Scripture; their country also is known, the places and rivers travelled unto and frequented by others, but to them an impenetrable rock, an inaccessible desert. Wherefore, if the Jews live, all the great wonders of old live in them, and then who can deny the stretched-out arm of a mighty God? especially since it may be a just doubt, whether considering the stubbornness of the nation, their living then in their country, under so many miracles, were a stranger thing than their present exile and disability to live in their country. And it is observable that this very thing was intended by God, that the Jews should be his proof and witnesses, as he calls them, *Isaiah* 43: 12. And their very dispersion in all lands was intended not only for a punishment to them, but for an exciting of others by their sight to the acknowledging of God, and his power, *Psalm* 59: 11. And therefore this kind of punishment was chosen rather than any other.

Thirdly, for grace: besides the continual succession (since the Gospel) of holy men, who have borne witness to the truth (there being no reason why any should distrust St. Luke, or Tertullian, or Chrysostom, more then Tully, Virgil, or Livy) there are two prophecies in the Gospel which evidently argue Christ's divinity by their success: the one concerning the woman that spent the ointment on our Saviour, for which he told that it should never be forgotten, but with the Gospel itself be preached to all ages, *Matthew* 26: 13; the other concerning the destruction of Jerusalem, of which our Saviour said that that generation should not pass till all were fulfilled, *Luke* 21: 32, which Josephus's History confirmeth, and the continuance of which verdict is yet evident. To these might be added the preaching of the Gospel in all nations, *Matthew* 24: 14, which we see even miraculously effected in these new discoveries, God turning men's covetousness and ambitions to the effecting of his word. Now, a prophecy is a wonder sent to posterity, lest they complain of want of wonders. It is a letter sealed and sent, which to the bearer is but paper, but to the receiver and opener is full of power. He that saw Christ open a blind man's eyes saw not more divinity than he that reads the woman's ointment in the Gospel or sees Jerusalem destroyed. With some of these heads enlarged, and woven into his discourse at several times and occasions, the parson settleth wavering minds. But if he sees them nearer desperation than atheism, not so much doubting a God, as that he is theirs, then he dives unto the boundless ocean of God's love and the unspeakable riches of his loving-kindness. He hath one argument unanswerable. If God hate them, either he doth it as they are creatures, dust and ashes, or as they are sinful. As creatures, he must needs love them; for no perfect artist ever yet hated his own work. As sinful, he must much more love them; because, notwithstanding his infinite hate of sin, his love overcame that hate; and with an exceeding great victory which in the creation needed not, gave them love for love, even the son of his love out of his bosom of love. So that man, which way soever he turns, hath two pledges of God's love, that in the mouth of two or three witnesses every word may be established: the one in his being, the other in his sinful being; and this as the more faulty in him, so the more glorious in God. And all may certainly conclude that God loves them, till either they despise that love or despair of his mercy; not any sin else but is within his love; but the despising of love must needs be without it. The thrusting away of his arm makes us only not embraced.

Conclusion

Many people look to the past for spiritual wisdom, particularly in writings that are widely considered to be spiritual classics. The works of George Herbert fall into this category. His poems in particular continue to be loved by a wide readership and from a literary perspective scholars number Herbert among the greatest English poets. The prose work *The Country Parson* is less well known to a general readership but continues to be studied as a masterpiece of ministerial spirituality and even a continuing model for pastoral care.

Of course, all classic texts, including spiritual classics, reflect and are limited by the assumptions of particular times and places. In the case of George Herbert, this is particularly apparent in his prose treatise *The Country Parson*. Today's readers are likely to be struck by the way Herbert's assumptions about social structures (not least a hierarchical class system) and about the Church separate the text from the present day. Despite the simplicity of Herbert's life in the parish (and recommendations of a simple life for parish priests), he came from an aristocratic and politically influential family. It is true that he warned priests against too close an association with local landowners or nobility but Herbert's parson is still in many ways patrician and paternalistic. At the same time, Herbert's Church, while influenced by the key elements of Reformation doctrine, was not wholly reformed in its hierarchical structure, including elements of its understanding of the status of the priest. The overwhelming impression given by *The Country Parson* is of a spirituality and approach to pastoral care that is tightly ordered and fairly clerical. The flavour of the whole is given in the telling phrase near the beginning of the book: 'A pastor is the deputy of Christ, for the reducing of man to the obedience of God.' The orderly life of the priest and his household; the right ordering of the church building; the good order of the parishioners; the maintenance of the proper order of society and of the state are no doubt capable of being seen as a kind of reflection of divine order. However, they also give the impression of a spirituality that is controlled and deeply institutional.

Herbert's country parson operates within a fixed social and religious order. As a result the priest exists in an ambiguous relationship with his parish. On the one hand he is to mix freely with parishioners, to eat with them on occasion or to entertain them in his own house. He is to view friendliness as a pastoral instrument. Yet the boundaries remain. The priest is socially and religiously removed from the rest of the village. He has an exclusive role in leading worship, in dispensing sacraments and in the key aspects of pastoral care. Herbert does not suggest a collaborative model of life and work except, in a limited way, in relation to the priest's wife and household. Hardly surprisingly, Herbert's model of pastoral care is also very masculine in an old-fashioned sense. Herbert's priest is a person of power, free standing and autonomous. His comments about the primacy of celibacy as well as about marriage and women appear to the contemporary reader as patriarchal. The parson and his household, however modestly they live, are people with servants, with financial means and with knowledge. Their role in relationship to parishioners is essentially parental. Even the parson's children and servants are drawn into this magic circle as dispensers of charity and spiritual wisdom to others.

A serious question therefore confronts the contemporary reader. Should *The Country Parson* nowadays be relegated to an antiquarian bookshelf as something of only historical interest? Is there a middle way between this and at best picking out the few parts that seem unquestionably acceptable to contemporary sensibilities while ignoring the structure of the whole? Equally, can Herbert's overall spiritual vision be redeemed for the present age?

Any contemporary reader must begin by honestly acknowledging that even a 'classic' religious text is not beyond criticism. In fact, the only way to approach such a text is in the light of one's own horizons of understanding and values because any contemporary reader also has a context which cannot be denied or escaped. Consequently, there needs to be a theory of interpretation that allows for a two-way conversation between the contemporary reader and a text from another age. In this conversation the wisdom of the text should be free to challenge the reader, even in its initial strangeness. Yet the contemporary reader must also be free to address critical questions to the text that arise from contemporary concerns and values. In that sense, the meaning of a text is never absolutely fixed or solely associated with the conscious intentions of the author or the author's original readership. In this way, further meaning may be found that was unavailable to an earlier generation – and indeed may not, indeed could not, have occurred to the original author.[1]

If we allow for a critical method of interpretation, how may George Herbert's spirituality still be accessible? A vital consideration is not to isolate works from each other within the same author's corpus. In this context, it is valid and important to place the poems of *The Temple* alongside *The Country Parson* when considering the richness and potential of Herbert's theology and spiritual vision. On its own, *The Country Parson* hardly suggests that priests share the same spiritual concerns as everyone else. The approach of the prose treatise is more austerely didactic than the poetry. Read in isolation, the emotional reticence of the treatise appears to emphasize detachment both in pastoral care and in personal spirituality. The honest self-exposure, inner struggle and spiritual depth of *The Temple*'s poetry provides a balance by revealing that passion and engagement also lay at the heart of George Herbert's life and ministry.

The use of poetry itself was also a means of communicating certain values. Subjectively, Herbert understood the writing of poetry to be a form of prayer and many of the poems of the central part of *The Temple* are in the form of familiar conversations with God or Christ. As a medium of teaching, the poetry does not have as its primary aim the communication of information about faith or of instructions for a moral or spiritual life. Compared to the language of *The Country Parson*, the language of Herbert's poetry has a rhetorical and evocative quality that more readily touches the emotions. It also has a particular capacity to unlock the imagination. Poetry is more capable of speaking of the mysterious, ambiguous and complex nature of faith. The value of Herbert's poetry as spiritual wisdom (and probably its conscious purpose), therefore, is to touch the reader in a more intimate way than the prose treatise and to provoke a deeper and more complex response.

Herbert and his circle in the Church of England espoused a relationship between beauty and holiness. The aesthetic power of poetry is one medium to express this relationship. Herbert appreciated that words must in the end give way to silence in the face of Mystery. They are

---

1 For a detailed treatment of interpretation theory (hermeneutics) in relation to classic spiritual texts, see P. Sheldrake, 'Interpretation' in A. Holder, ed., *The Blackwell Companion to Christian Spirituality*, Part VI: Special Topics, Oxford: Blackwell Publishing 2005.

always at the service of wonder. With art, music and ritual, poetry has a special power to move towards the boundary of contemplative awareness.

Clearly the spiritual values that George Herbert proposes are based on life in the Christian Church and participation in Christian worship. Equally, even within a Church context, a strong emphasis on the centrality of a single set form of liturgy, the *Book of Common Prayer*, may distance Herbert's perspectives from many contemporary Christians as it did from his Puritan contemporaries. However, Herbert's approach reminds the contemporary reader that it is important not to reduce the meaning of 'spirituality' to a matter of individual choices or to the inner life of individuals in isolation. In Christian terms, spirituality always concerns the nurturing of a community of faith, worship, charity and engagement with a wider social world.

Taken as a whole, Herbert's spirituality describes a way of living and a network of relationships rather than a set of abstract theories. Equally, his spiritual vision embraces every aspect of everyday human life, not simply the obviously religious dimensions. In contemporary language this might be described as holistic. Consequently, when read with critical care, many of the spiritual values that emerge from Herbert's writings continue to be accessible to people in vastly different eras and circumstances. Ultimately, George Herbert's writings offer spiritual wisdom that many people still find engaging precisely because he understood and evoked the depths of the human heart with insight and sensitivity.

Further Reading

Editions

The following are modern editions of *The Temple* and *The Country Parson*.

John N. Hall, ed., *George Herbert – The Country Parson, The Temple*, The Classics of Western Spirituality, New York: Paulist Press, 1981.

Louis L. Martz, ed., *George Herbert and Henry Vaughan*, The Oxford Authors, Oxford/New York: Oxford University Press, 1986.

Ann Pasternak Slater, ed., *George Herbert: The Complete English Works*, Everyman's Library 204, London: David Campbell Publishers, 1995. The Introduction is particularly good on manuscript questions.

Isaak Walton's Life

The classic seventeenth-century *The Life of Mr George Herbert* by Isaak Walton appears as Appendix 3 of the Pasternak Slater edition of Herbert's works.

Anglican Spiritual Tradition

For general studies of spirituality in the Anglican tradition, see:

A. M. Allchin, 'Anglican Spirituality' in S. Sykes and J. Booty, eds., *The Study of Anglicanism*, London: SPCK/Minneapolis: Fortress Press, 1988.

A. Bartlett, *A Passionate Balance: The Anglican Tradition*, London: Darton Longman and Todd/New York: Orbis Books, 2007.

W. Countryman, *The Poetic Imagination: An Anglican Spiritual Tradition*, London: Darton Longman and Todd/New York: Orbis Books, 1999.

G. Rowell, K. Stephenson and R. Williams, eds., *Love's Redeeming Work: The Anglican Quest for Holiness*, Oxford: Oxford University Press, 2001.

Studies of George Herbert

The following is a small selection of studies about George Herbert, his writings, theology and spirituality.

Elizabeth Clarke, *Theory and Theology in George Herbert's Poetry: 'Divinitie, and Poesie, Met'*, Oxford: Clarendon Press, 1997.

Arthur L. Clements, *Poetry of Contemplation: John Donne, George Herbert, Henry Vaughan and the Modern Period*, New York: State University of New York Press, 1990.

R. W. Cooley, *Full of All Knowledge: George Herbert's Country Parson and Early Modern Social Discourse*, Toronto: University of Toronto Press, 2004.

C. Hodgkin, *Authority, Church and Society in George Herbert*, Columbia: University of Missouri Press, 1993.

B. Lewalski, *Protestant Poetics and the Seventeenth-Century Religious Lyric*, Princeton: Princeton University Press, 1979.

L. Martz, *The Poetry of Meditation: A Study of English Religious Literature of the Seventeenth Century*, New Haven: Yale University Press, 1954.

Richard Strier, *Love Known: Theology and Experience in George Herbert's Poetry*, Chicago: University of Chicago Press, 1986.

J. H. Summers, *George Herbert: His Religion and Art*, Medieval and Renaissance Texts and Studies: Binghamton, New York: Center for Medieval and Early Renaissance Studies, 1981.

S. Sykes, *Unashamed Anglicanism*, London: Darton Longman and Todd, 1999, Chapter 3.

Rosamund Tuve, *A Reading of George Herbert*, Chicago: University of Chicago Press [1952], reprint 1982.

Gene E. Veith, *Reformation Spirituality: The Religion of George Herbert*, London and Toronto: Associated University Presses, 1985.

General Index

Index of Readings